Sunbeam Snakes as Pets.

Sunbeam Snake Facts and Information.

Sunbeam Snake Care, Behavior, Diet, Interaction, Costs and Health.

By

Ben Team

ALL RIGHTS RESERVED. This book contains material protected under International and Federal Copyright Laws and Treaties.

Any unauthorized reprint or use of this material is strictly prohibited. No part of this book may be reproduced or transmitted in any form or by any means, electronic, mechanical or otherwise, including photocopying or recording, or by any information storage and retrieval system without express written permission from the author.

Copyright © 2018

Published by: Zoodoo Publishing

Table of Contents

About the Author 5

Foreword 5

PART I: THE SUNBEAM SNAKE 8

Chapter 1: Sunbeam Snake Description and Anatomy 9

Chapter 2: Sunbeam Snake Biology and Behavior 15

Chapter 3: Classification and Taxonomy 19

Chapter 4: The Sunbeam Snake's World 20

PART II: SUNBEAM SNAKE HUSBANDRY 21

Chapter 5: Sunbeam Snakes as Pets 22

Chapter 6: Providing the Captive Habitat 36

Chapter 7: Heating the Habitat 43

Chapter 8: Enclosure Furniture 56

Chapter 9: Substrates 61

Chapter 10: Maintaining the Captive Habitat 65

Chapter 11: Feeding Sunbeam Snakes 73

Chapter 12: Providing Water to Your Sunbeam Snake 76

Chapter 13: Interacting with Your Sunbeam Snake 79

Chapter 14: Common Health Concerns 83

Chapter 15: Breeding Sunbeam Snakes 95

Chapter 16: Further Reading 105

References **111**

Index **113**

About the Author

The author, Ben Team, is an environmental educator and author with over 16 years of professional reptile-keeping experience. Ben currently maintains www.FootstepsInTheForest.com, where he shares information, narration and observations of the natural world.

Foreword

Many of the most popular pet snake species have been kept by reptile enthusiasts for decades. This includes corn snakes, ball pythons, boa constrictors and kingsnakes, among others.

Over that time, keepers have developed husbandry regimens that suit these species, thereby removing most of the guesswork from the equation. Even beginners are usually able to maintain these snakes without problem.

Many of these snakes are even bred regularly in captivity, which makes captive-bred offspring available to hobbyists. This is quite helpful for those who'd like to keep these species, as captive-bred offspring are superior to their wild-caught counterparts in almost all respects.

Indeed, there's little reason for keepers to even consider purchasing wild-caught corn or king snakes.

But a handful of popular species have proven more difficult. Some have unusual biological needs, while others simply don't adapt well to captivity.

In most cases, keepers eventually figure out the best recipe for captive maintenance. But there's a big difference between figuring out how to keep a difficult species alive and devising a method for inducing captive reproduction.

Sunbeam snakes are a great example of this phenomenon. They're relatively common in the snake-keeping hobby, and a relatively straightforward husbandry regimen has been developed for those who wish to keep them. However, they've yet to be bred regularly. A few hobbyists have had luck from time to time, but regular breedings have proven elusive.

Accordingly, the only sunbeam snakes available to hobbyists are wild-caught individuals. Some hobbyist will eventually crack the code and figure out the things necessary to induce captive reproduction, but thus far, such attempts have largely fallen short.

***

Because captive bred individuals aren't widely available, sunbeam snakes have developed a bit of a reputation for being difficult to maintain.

And while it is true that sunbeam snakes aren't as easy to keep as corn snakes or ball pythons are, they aren't particularly difficult to care for, either.

In fact, they can make very good pets. Aside from their need for very high humidity levels and secrecy, their care requirements don't differ very much from those of most other snakes.

They're fantastically beautiful and interesting captives. Their skin displays a beautiful iridescence, which is unmatched by many other species, and they're generally quite docile when handled. They are also easy to feed – something that should never be taken for granted with wild-caught snakes.

In fact, they are one of the few wild-caught species that is suitable for relatively inexperienced keepers. They aren't an ideal first snake, but keepers who've already kept one or two other snakes will likely find success is attainable.

You simply need to provide them with the things they need to thrive and work closely with your vet upon acquiring a sunbeam snake, as they'll frequently bear high parasite loads. However, these types of problems are often easy to solve.

***

Sunbeam snakes certainly aren't ideal for all keepers. They don't like being handled very much, they're very secretive and because they're not as commonly kept as many other species, it can be difficult to find information about them.

However, those who don't mind these challenges will likely find that sunbeam snakes are fascinating captives, who make rewarding – if occasionally challenging – pets.

The trick is to learn as much as you can about these snakes, the habitats from which they hail, and the techniques other keepers have found helpful.

And you can begin doing exactly that on the following pages.

PART I: THE SUNBEAM SNAKE

Properly caring for any animal requires an understanding of the species and its place in the natural world. This includes digesting subjects as disparate as anatomy and ecology, diet and geography, and reproduction and physiology.

It is only by learning what your pet is, how it lives, what it does that you can achieve the primary goal of animal husbandry: Providing your pet with the highest quality of life possible.

Chapter 1: Sunbeam Snake Description and Anatomy

Like most other snakes, sunbeam snakes (*Xenopeltis unicolor*) have evolved a number of morphological adaptations to help them survive.

But although they exhibit a few anatomical peculiarities, sunbeam snakes possess a fairly typical body plan, which resembles that of most other snakes.

Size

Sunbeam snakes are average sized snakes, and most adults reach lengths of between 36 and 48 inches (90 to 120 centimeters). Occasional specimens may exceed 50 inches (127 centimeters) in length, but such giants are quite rare.

Adult sunbeam snakes weigh about 20 to 28 ounces (600 to 800 grams), although this can vary depending on their body condition and length. The largest individuals probably approach 35 ounces (1 kilogram).

Hatchling sunbeam snakes are poorly known, but the hatchlings are likely about 6 to 8 inches long (15 to 20 centimeters).

Sunbeam snakes are sexually dimorphic with respect to size, as the females reach slightly larger sizes than the males do.

Scalation

Sunbeam snakes are covered in very distinctive scales. They are remarkably smooth, highly polished and produce an iridescence that must be seen to be believed. The scales fit together tightly, and they feel very smooth to the touch.

These scales likely help to reduce friction, thereby helping the snakes to burrow through the substrate. They may also help the snakes camouflage better from predators, as the iridescence helps them blend in with the moisture present under rocks and logs. This way, if a predator lifts up a rock, the snake is less likely to be seen beneath it.

The ventral scales of sunbeam snakes are wide and help propel the snakes across the ground, while the scales on the sides and back of the snakes are small and somewhat hexagonal.

Color and Pattern

Sunbeam snakes are essentially unicolored dorsally (hence their scientific name). Most specimens are clad in some shade of brown, grey or black, which can look different depending on the light in which the snake is viewed. .

There is no discernible pattern present, although the light-colored skin between the scales is sometimes visible, which gives the snakes a chain-link appearance.

The belly of sunbeam snakes is white to off-yellow and varies from one individual to the next.

Hatchling sunbeam snakes bear a light-colored marking behind the head, but it fades within a few weeks.

Body, Head and Tail

Sunbeam snakes have relatively thick bodies for their size. They have very short tails, which represent less than 10% of their total length. This is probably an adaptation that helps provide the snakes with a stable base that can be used to help push the snakes forward.

Their heads are slightly flattened and chisel-shaped, which is likely an adaptation that facilitates burrowing. The eyes and nostrils of sunbeam snakes are quite small, both of which are likely adaptations that suit their burrowing lifestyle.

The sunbeam snake has a slightly different skull than most advanced snakes. They are unable to open their mouths as wide as many other snakes can, although they can still consume relatively large prey (although they cannot ingest gigantic meals like many boas and pythons can).

They also have hinged teeth. This is thought to be an adaptation that enables them to catch and consume hard-bodied prey, such as lizards and snakes.

Vent

Like all other snakes, sunbeam snakes possess a vent at the base of their tail. Located on the ventral side of the body, the vent serves as the exit point for urates and feces. It is also the place from which the hemipenes of males and the eggs produced by females emerge.

Internal Organs

The internal anatomy of sunbeam snakes differs relatively little from that of other snakes.

Sunbeam snakes draw oxygen in through their nostrils; pipe it through the trachea and into the lungs. Here, blood exchanges carbon dioxide for oxygen, before it is pumped to the various body parts via the heart and blood vessels.

Sunbeam snakes can vary from brown to black in color.

While the hearts of sunbeam snakes feature only three true chambers (two atria and a single ventricle), a septum keeps the ventricle divided at most times, allowing the heart to operate similarly to a four-chambered, mammalian heart.

This means that in practice, sunbeam snakes keep their oxygenated and deoxygenated blood relatively separate in the heart.

Their digestive system is comprised of an esophagus, stomach, small intestine, large intestine and a terminal chamber called the cloaca. The stomach has considerable ability to stretch and accommodate food.

The liver resides near the center of the animal's torso, with the gallbladder sitting directly behind it. While the gallbladder stores bile, the liver provides a number of functions relating to digestion, metabolism and filtration.

Kidneys, which lie almost directly behind the lungs, filter wastes from the snake's bloodstream.

Like other snakes, sunbeam snakes control their bodies via their brain and nervous system. Their endocrine and exocrine glands work much as they do in other vertebrates.

Reproductive Organs

Like all squamates, male sunbeam snakes have paired reproductive organs, called hemipenes. When not in use, males keep their hemipenes inside the bases of their tails. When they attempt to mate with a female, they evert one of the hemipenes and insert it into the female's cloaca.

The paired nature of the male sex organs ensures that males can continue to breed if they suffer an injury to one of the hemipenes. This paired arrangement also allows male sunbeam snakes to mate with females on either side of their body.

Females have paired ovaries, which produce ova (eggs), and they have paired oviducts, which store the eggs after they are released from the ovaries.

The eggs are shelled and held inside the oviducts until it is time to deposit the eggs. At this time, the eggs are passed from the oviducts into the cloaca and out of the body via the vent.

Chapter 2: Sunbeam Snake Biology and Behavior

Sunbeam snakes exhibit a number of biological and behavioral adaptations that allow them to survive in their natural habitats.

Shedding

Like other scaled reptiles, sunbeam snakes shed their old skin to reveal new, fresh skin underneath. Shedding may occur as often as every two to four weeks or as infrequently as twice as year. The rate at which a snake sheds largely depends on its growth rate, although stress, illness and injury may also trigger rapid shed cycles.

Ideally, sunbeam snakes shed in one long, full piece. However, dehydration and injuries can cause a sunbeam snake to shed in several separate pieces. Most sunbeam snakes are often incredibly iridescent immediately following a shed.

Metabolism and Digestion

Sunbeam snakes are ectothermic ("cold-blooded") animals, whose internal metabolism depends on their body temperature. When warm, their bodily functions proceed more rapidly; when cold, their bodily functions proceed slowly.

This also means that the snakes digest more effectively at suitably warm temperatures than they do at suboptimal temperatures. Their appetites also vary with temperature, and if the temperatures drop below the preferred range, they may cease feeding entirely.

A sunbeam snake's body temperature largely follows ambient air temperatures, but they also absorb and reflect radiant heat, such as that coming from the sun. The snakes try to keep their body temperature within the preferred range by employing behaviors that allow them to adjust their temperature.

For example, sunbeam snakes bask to raise their temperature when they are too cool. Alternatively, when it is necessary to cool off, sunbeam snakes may move into cooler soil or venture deeper underground to escape the heat.

Growth Rate and Lifespan

Little is known about the growth rate and lifespan of sunbeam snakes.

Sunbeam snakes appear to have a relatively typical growth rate, based on the few young individuals that have been kept in captivity. Most will likely require between 2 and 4 years to reach maturity.

They can likely live for at least 5 to 8 years, and maybe as long as 10 – perhaps longer. As with most other medium-sized snakes, many probably perish at the hands of predators before reaching their first birthday.

Foraging Behavior

Unlike some other snakes, which ambush prey that strays too close, sunbeam snakes are thought to forage actively. They typically prowl through loose substrates, shallow water and surface debris, where they seek small vertebrate prey, including frogs, snakes and rodents.

Sunbeam snakes are not venomous; they constrict their prey in the same basic way pythons and rat snakes do. However, they may swallow very small prey live, without constricting it.

Diel and Seasonal Activity

As with many other aspects of sunbeam snake behavior and biology, little is known about their daily and seasonal patterns.

They appear to be almost entirely nocturnal, animals who spend their days hiding beneath the substrate. They often crawl across the surface at night, to search for food and seek mates.

Sunbeam snakes can likely remain active all year long, as they are native to southeast Asia. However, they are clearly imported seasonally, which suggests that they are likely more active in some parts of the year than others.

Captive individuals will thrive on a consistent yearly schedule, although seasonal temperature fluctuations may help trigger breeding behaviors.

Defensive Strategies and Tactics

Crypsis is the first method by which sunbeam snakes seek to defend themselves. Their iridescent scales blend and secretive habits make them quite difficult for predators to locate.

When crypsis fails, sunbeam snakes may remain motionless or try to flee. They rarely bite if captured, but they will exude a foul-smelling musk from glands in their tails.

Some keepers have suggested that they vibrate their tails if frightened, but others report never seeing the behavior, despite extensive experience with the species.

Reproduction

Virtually nothing is known of the breeding habits of sunbeam snakes. They are an egg-laying species and they are thought to produce clutches of between 6 and 12 eggs.

Chapter 3: Classification and Taxonomy

Like all other living species, sunbeam snakes are placed within a hierarchical classification scheme. The highest levels of this classification scheme help distinguish groups like vertebrates from others, while the lower levels of classification distinguish sunbeam snakes from other snakes.

As currently construed, the sunbeam snake's classification scheme is as follows:

Kingdom: Animalia

Phylum: Chordata

Class: Reptilia

Order: Squamata

Family: Xenopeltidae

Genus: *Xenopeltis*

Scientists currently recognize two different species within the genus *Xenopeltis*.

- *Xenopeltis unicolors* – Sunbeam Snake

- *Xenopeltis hainanensis* – Chinese Sunbeam Snake

The Chinese sunbeam snake is rather poorly known and it is not commonly seen for sale.

Chapter 4: The Sunbeam Snake's World

Sunbeam snakes combine to range across a relatively wide geographic area, and they inhabit a number of different habitats.

Range

The exact range of the sunbeam snake is not well defined, but they generally range throughout southeast Asia, including several island groups in the Indian Ocean.

In the west, they are found in Myanmar, and they also inhabit the Andaman and Nicobar Islands. Their range extends eastward through southern China, Laos, Thailand and Vietnam, and it continues all the way into the Philippines.

They range southward into Cambodia and Malaysia, and they are even found throughout much of Indonesia, including the Greater Sunda Islands.

Climate and Habitat

Sunbeam snakes are relatively adaptable serpents, who inhabit a range of different habitats.

Most sunbeam snakes prefer to live in damp forests, marshes, riparian areas, mountain valleys and swamps. However, they also inhabit disturbed areas, such as agricultural regions and neighborhood gardens.

Sunbeam snakes typically inhabit low-lying areas, but they have been recorded at elevations of up to 4,200 feet above sea level (1,300 meters).

PART II: SUNBEAM SNAKE HUSBANDRY

Once equipped with a basic understanding of what sunbeam snakes *are* (Chapter 1 and Chapter 3), where they *live* (Chapter 4), and what they *do* (Chapter 2) you can begin learning about their captive care.

Animal husbandry is an evolving pursuit. Keepers shift their strategies frequently as they incorporate new information and ideas into their husbandry paradigms.

There are few "right" or "wrong" answers, and what works in one situation may not work in another. Accordingly, you may find that different authorities present different, and sometimes conflicting, information regarding the care of these snakes.

In all cases, you must strive to learn as much as you can about your pet and its natural habitat, so that you may provide it with the best quality of life possible.

Chapter 5: Sunbeam Snakes as Pets

Sunbeam snakes can make rewarding pets, but you must know what to expect before adding one to your home. This includes not only understanding the nature of the care they require but also the costs associated with this care.

Assuming that you feel confident in your ability to care for a sunbeam snake and endure the associated financial burdens, you can begin seeking your individual pet.

Understanding the Commitment

Keeping a sunbeam snake as a pet requires a substantial commitment. You will be responsible for your pet's well-being for the rest of its life. Sunbeam snakes often live for 5 years or more, and you must be prepared to care for your new pet for this entire time.

Can you be sure that you will still want to care for your pet several years in the future? Do you know what your living situation will be? What changes will have occurred in your family? How will your working life have changed over this time?

You must consider all of these possibilities before acquiring a new pet. Failing to do so often leads to apathy, neglect and even resentment, which is not good for you or your pet sunbeam snake.

Neglecting your pet is wrong, and in some locations, a criminal offense. You must continue to provide quality care for your sunbeam snakes, even once the novelty has worn off, and it is no longer fun to clean the cage and provide him with insects each week.

Once you purchase a sunbeam snake, its well-being becomes your responsibility until it passes away at the end of a long life, or you have found someone who will agree to adopt the animal for you. Unfortunately, this is rarely an easy task. You may begin with thoughts of selling your pet to help recoup a small part of your investment, but these efforts will largely fall flat.

While professional breeders may profit from the sale of sunbeam snakes, amateurs are at a decided disadvantage. Only a tiny sliver of the general population is interested in reptilian pets, and only a small subset of these are interested in keeping sunbeam snakes.

Of those who are interested in acquiring a sunbeam snake, most would rather start fresh, by *purchasing* a small hatchling or juvenile from an established breeder, rather than adopting your questionable animal *for free*.

After having difficulty finding a willing party to purchase or adopt your animal, many owners try to donate their pet to a local zoo. Unfortunately, this rarely works either.

Zoos are not interested in your sunbeam snake, no matter how pretty he is. He is a pet with little to no reliable provenance and questionable health status. This is simply not the type of animal zoos are eager to add to their multi-million-dollar collections.

Zoos obtain most of their animals from other zoos and museums; failing that, they obtain their animals directly from their land of origin. As a rule, they do not accept donated pets.

No matter how difficult it becomes to find a new home for your unwanted sunbeam snake, you must never release non-native reptiles into the wild.

Additionally, released or escaped reptiles cause a great deal of distress to those who are frightened by them. This leads local municipalities to adopt pet restrictions or ban reptile keeping entirely.

The Costs of Captivity

Reptiles are often marketed as low-cost pets. While true in a relative sense (the costs associated with dog, cat, horse or tropical fish husbandry are often much higher than they are for sunbeam snakes), potential keepers must still prepare for the financial implications of snake ownership.

At the outset, you must budget for the acquisition of your pet, as well as the costs of purchasing or constructing a habitat. Unfortunately, while many keepers plan for these costs, they typically fail to consider the on-going costs, which will quickly eclipse the initial startup costs.

Startup Costs

One surprising fact most new keepers learn is the enclosure and equipment will often cost as much as (or more than) the animal does (except in the case of very high-priced specimens).

Prices fluctuate from one market to the next, but in general, the least you will spend on a healthy sunbeam snake is about $25 (£18); you'll also need to spend another $50 (£36) on his initial habitat and care equipment. Replacement equipment and food will represent additional (and ongoing) expenses.

Ongoing Costs

The ongoing costs of sunbeam snake ownership primarily fall into one of three categories: food, maintenance and veterinary care.

Food costs are the most significant of the three, but they are relatively consistent and somewhat predictable. Some maintenance costs are easy to calculate, but things like equipment malfunctions are impossible to predict with any certainty. Veterinary expenses are hard to predict and vary wildly from one year to the next.

Food Costs

Food is the single greatest ongoing cost you will experience while caring for your sunbeam snake. To obtain a reasonable estimate of your yearly food costs, you must consider the number of meals you will feed your pet per year and the cost of each meal.

The amount of food your sunbeam snake will consume will vary based on numerous factors, including his size, the average temperatures in his habitat and his health.

As a ballpark number, you should figure that you'll need about $2 (£1.50) per week – roughly $100 (£70) per year -- for food. You could certainly spend more or less than this, but that is a reasonable estimate for back-of-the-envelope calculations.

Veterinary Costs

While you should always seek veterinary advice at the first sign of illness, it is probably not wise to haul your healthy sunbeam snake to the vet's office for no reason – they don't require "checkups" or annual vaccinations as some other pets may. Accordingly, you shouldn't incur any veterinary expenses unless your pet falls ill.

However, veterinary care can become very expensive, very quickly. In addition to a basic exam or phone consultation, your sunbeam snake may need cultures, x-rays or other diagnostic tests performed. In light of this, wise keepers budget at least $200 to $300 (£160 to £245) each year to cover any emergency veterinary costs.

Maintenance Costs

It is important to plan for both routine and unexpected maintenance costs. Commonly used items, such as paper towels, disinfectant and topsoil are rather easy to calculate. However, it is not easy to know how many burned out light bulbs, cracked misting units or faulty thermostats you will have to replace in a given year.

Those who keep their sunbeam snake in simple enclosures will find that about $50 (£40) covers their yearly maintenance costs. By contrast, those who maintain elaborate habitats may spend $200 (£160) or more each year.

Always try to purchase frequently used supplies, such as light bulbs, paper towels and disinfectants in bulk to maximize your savings. It is often beneficial to consult with local reptile-keeping clubs, who often pool their resources to attain greater buying power.

Myths and Misunderstandings

Unfortunately, there are many myths and misunderstandings about sunbeam snakes and reptile-keeping in general. Some myths represent outdated thinking or techniques, while other myths and misunderstandings reflect the desires of keepers, rather than the reality of the situation.

Myth: *Sunbeam snakes will only grow to the size of their enclosure, and then they stop growing entirely.*

Fact: Despite the popularity of this myth, healthy snakes do not stop growing until they reach their mature, adult size. Keeping a sunbeam snake in an inappropriately small cage is an inhumane practice that will only lead to a stressed, sick animal.

Myth: *Sunbeam snakes are reptiles, so they are not capable of suffering or feeling pain.*

Fact: While it is important to avoid anthropomorphizing or projecting human emotions and motivations to non-human entities, reptiles – including sunbeam snakes – feel pain. There is no doubt that they can experience pain and seek to avoid it.

While it is impossible to know exactly what a sunbeam snake thinks, there is no reason to believe that they do not suffer similarly to other animals, when injured, ill or depressed.

Myth: *My sunbeam snake likes to be held so he can feel the warmth of my hands.*

Fact: In truth, your sunbeam snake may tolerate being held, but it probably does not "like" it. This myth springs from the notion that because reptiles are "cold-blooded," and they must derive their heat from external sources, they must enjoy warmth at all times. However, this is an oversimplification of their behavior.

Myth: *Sunbeam snakes are good pets for young children.*

Fact: While many reptiles, including sunbeam snakes, make wonderful pets for adults, teenagers and families, they require more care than a young child can provide. The age at which a child is capable of caring for a pet will vary, but children should be about 10 to 12 years of age before they are allowed to care for their own sunbeam snake. Parents must exercise prudent judgment and make a sound assessment of their child's capabilities and maturity. Children will certainly enjoy pet reptiles, but they must be cared for by someone with adequate maturity. Additionally, it is important to consider the potential for young children contracting salmonella and other pathogens from the family pet.

Myth: *If you get tired of a sunbeam snake, it is easy to find a new home for it. The zoo will surely want your pet; after all, you are* *giving it to them free of charge! If that doesn't work, you can always just release it into the wild.*

Fact: Acquiring a pet sunbeam snake is a very big commitment. If you ever decide that your pet no longer fits your family or lifestyle, you may have a tough time finding a suitable home for it. You can attempt to sell the animal, but this is illegal in some places, and often requires a permit or license to do legally.

Zoos and pet stores will be reticent to accept your pet – even at no charge – because they cannot be sure that your pet does not have an illness that could spread through their collections. A zoo may have to spend hundreds or thousands of dollars for the care, housing and veterinary care to accept your pet sunbeam snake, and such things are not taken lightly.

Some people consider releasing their sunbeam snake into the wild if no other accommodations can be made, but such acts are destructive, often illegal and usually a death sentence for the snake.

Even if you live in the sunbeam snake's natural range, captive animals should never be released into the wild, as they can spread pathogens that may wipe out a native population. You will likely have to solicit the help of a rescue group or shelter devoted to reptiles in finding a new home for an unwanted pet.

Acquiring Your Sunbeam Snake

Modern reptile enthusiasts can acquire sunbeam snakes from a variety of sources, each with a different set of pros and cons.

Pet stores are one of the first places many people see sunbeam snakes, and they become the de facto source of pets for many beginning keepers. While they do offer some unique benefits to prospective keepers, pet stores are not always the best place to purchase a pet snake; so, consider all of the available options, including breeders and reptile swap meets, before making a purchase.

Pet Stores

Pet stores offer a number of benefits to keepers shopping for sunbeam snakes, including convenience: They usually stock all of the equipment your new snake needs, including cages, heating devices and food items.

Additionally, they offer you the chance to inspect the sunbeam snake up close before purchase. In some cases, you may be able to choose from more than one specimen. Many pet stores provide health guarantees for a short period, which provide some recourse if your new pet turns out to be ill.

However, pet stores are not always the ideal place to purchase your new pet. Pet stores are retail establishments, and as such, you will usually pay more for your new pet than you would from a breeder.

Additionally, pet stores rarely know the pedigree of the animals they sell, and they will rarely know the sunbeam snake's date of birth or other pertinent information.

Other drawbacks associated with pet stores primarily relate to the staff's inexperience. While some pet stores concentrate on reptiles and may educate their staff about proper sunbeam snake care, many others provide incorrect advice to their customers.

It is also worth considering the increased exposure to pathogens that pet store animals endure, given the constant flow of animals through such facilities.

Reptile Expos

Reptile expos offer another option for purchasing sunbeam snakes. Reptile expos often feature resellers, breeders and retailers in the same room, all selling various types of sunbeam snakes and other reptiles.

Often, the prices at such events are quite reasonable and you are often able to select from many different sunbeam snakes. However, if you have a problem, it may be difficult to find the seller after the event is over.

Breeders

Because they usually offer unparalleled information and support to their customers, breeders are the ideal place to shop for sunbeam snakes. Additionally, breeders often know the species well and are better able to help you learn the husbandry techniques necessary for success.

But unfortunately, sunbeam snakes are very rarely bred in captivity. This means that it is rarely possible to purchase them from a breeder. Nevertheless, it is always preferable to purchase captive bred offspring whenever you can find them.

The primary disadvantage of buying from a breeder is that you must often make such purchases from a distance, either by phone or via the internet. Nevertheless, most established breeders are happy to provide you with photographs of the animal you will be purchasing, as well as his or her parents.

Selecting Your Sunbeam Snake

Not all sunbeam snakes are created equally, so it is important to select a healthy individual that will give you the best chance of success.

Practically speaking, the most important criterion to consider is the health of the animal. However, the sex and history of the sunbeam snake are also important things to consider.

Health Checklist

Always check your sunbeam snake thoroughly for signs of injury or illness before purchasing it. If you are purchasing the animal from someone in a different part of the country, you must inspect it immediately upon delivery. Notify the seller promptly if the animal exhibits any health problems.

Avoid the temptation to acquire or accept a sick or injured animal in hopes of nursing him back to health. Not only are you likely to incur substantial veterinary costs while treating your new pet, you will likely fail in your attempts to restore the sunbeam snake to full health. Sick animals rarely recover in the hands of novices.

Additionally, by purchasing injured or diseased animals, you incentivize poor husbandry on the part of the retailer. If retailers lose money on sick or injured animals, they will take steps to avoid this eventuality, by acquiring healthier stock in the first place and providing better care for their charges.

As much as is possible, try to observe the following features:

- **Observe the animal's skin**. It should be free of lacerations and other damage. Pay special attention to those areas that frequently sustain damage, such as the tail and the front of the face. A small cut or abrasion may be relatively easy to treat, but significant abrasions and cuts are likely to become infected and require significant treatment.

- **Gently check the animal's crevices and creases for mites and ticks**. Avoid purchasing any animal that has ectoparasites. Additionally, you should avoid purchasing any other animals from this source, as they are likely to harbor parasites as well.

- **Examine the animal's eyes and nostrils**. The eyes should not be sunken, and they should be free of discharge. The nostrils should be clear and dry – snakes with runny noses or those who blow bubbles are likely to be suffering from a respiratory infection.

- **Gently palpate the animal and ensure no lumps or anomalies are apparent**. Lumps in the muscles or abdominal cavity may indicate parasites, abscesses or tumors.

- **Observe the animal's demeanor**. Healthy sunbeam snakes are aware of their environment and react to stimuli. When active, the animal should calmly explore his environment. Avoid lethargic animals, which do not appear alert.

- **Check the animal's vent.** The vent should be clean and free of smeared feces. Smeared feces can indicate parasites or bacterial infections.

The Sex

Unless you are attempting to breed sunbeam snakes, you should select a male pet, as females are more likely to suffer from reproduction-related health problems than males are.

Some females will produce and deposit (infertile) egg clutches upon reaching maturity, whether they are housed with a male or not. While this is not necessarily problematic, novices can easily avoid this unnecessary complication by selecting males as pets.

Quarantine

Because new animals may have illnesses or parasites that could infect the rest of your collection, it is wise to quarantine all new acquisitions. This means that you should keep any new animal as separated from the rest of your pets as possible. Only once you have ensured that the new animal is healthy should you introduce it to the rest of your collection.

During the quarantine period, you should keep the new sunbeam snake in a simplified habitat, with a paper substrate, water bowl, several branches, basking spot and a few hiding places. Keep the temperature and humidity at ideal levels.

It is wise to obtain fecal samples from your sunbeam snake during the quarantine period. You can take these samples to your veterinarian, who can check them for signs of internal parasites. Always treat any existing parasite infestations before removing the animal from quarantine.

Always tend to quarantined animals last, as this reduces the chances of transmitting pathogens to your healthy animals. Do not wash quarantined water bowls or cage furniture with those belonging to your healthy animals. Whenever possible, use completely separate tools for quarantined animals and those that have been in your collection for some time.

Always be sure to wash your hands thoroughly after handling quarantined animals, their cages or their tools. Particularly careful keepers wear a smock or alternative clothing when handling quarantined animals.

Quarantine new acquisitions for a minimum of 30 days; 60 or 90 days is even better. Many zoos and professional breeders maintain 180- or 360-day-long quarantine periods.

Chapter 6: Providing the Captive Habitat

Providing your sunbeam snake with appropriate housing is and essential aspect of captive care. In essence, the habitat you provide to your snake becomes his "world."

In "the old days," those inclined to keep snakes had few choices with regard to caging. The two primary options were to build a custom cage from scratch or construct a lid to use with a fish aquarium.

By contrast, modern hobbyists have a variety of options from which to choose. In addition to building custom cages or adapting aquaria, dozens of different cage styles are available – each with different pros and cons.

Dimensions

Throughout their lives, snakes need a cage large enough to lay comfortably, access a range of temperatures and get enough room for exercise.

A good rule of thumb is to ensure that the snake is no longer than ½ of the cage's perimeter.

For example, a 55-gallon aquarium is about 48 inches long by 12 inches deep. This means that the perimeter of the aquarium is about 120 inches long, or 10 feet. Half of this is 60 inches, meaning that such an aquarium could comfortably house a 5-foot-long snake – more than enough space to accommodate even the largest sunbeam snake.

By way of another example, consider that a 10-gallon aquarium is about 20 inches long, by 11 inches wide. With a perimeter of 62 inches, the cage is suitable for a snake that is about 31 inches long.

In practice, most adult sunbeam snakes will require a habitat in the 20- to 40-gallon range, or roughly 30 inches by 12 inches to 36 inches by 18 inches.

Remember, this rule is a guideline for the *minimum* amount of space your snake requires. Always strive to offer the largest cage that you reasonably can. While many keepers suggest that large cages are intimidating to snakes, the truth is more subtle. Contrary to the popular notion, large cages – in and of themselves – do not cause snakes to experience stress.

Snakes live in habitats that exceed even the largest cages by several orders of magnitude. What snakes do not do, however, is spend much time exposed. Large, barren cages that do not feature complex cage props and numerous hiding places may very well stress snakes. However, large, complex habitats afford more space for exercising and exploring in addition to allowing for the establishment of a superb thermal gradient.

In addition to total space, the layout of the cage is also important – rectangular cages are strongly preferable for a variety of reasons:

- They allow the keeper to establish more drastic heat gradients.

- Cages with one long direction allow your snake to stretch out better than square cage do.

- Front opening cages are easier to maintain when the cages are rectangular, as you do not have to reach as far back into the cage to reach the back wall.

Security

While sunbeam snakes are typically considered harmless animals, it is extremely important to consider cage security. They are escape artists – if it is possible to escape from the cage, they eventually will. In most circumstances, if a snake can push its head through a crack, it can usually pull its entire body behind it.

Never use a cage to house a sunbeam snake if you are not certain that it is escape proof. Additionally, be sure to inspect all cages regularly to catch problems (such as a fraying bit of screen or a loose door gasket) before they are large enough to permit the snake to escape.

Aquariums

Aquariums are popular choices for snake cages, largely because of their ubiquity. Virtually any pet store that carries snakes also stocks aquariums.

Aquariums can make suitable snake cages, but they have a number of drawbacks. For starters, glass cages are hard to clean, and they are easy to break while you are carrying them around. Aquariums that are large are likely to be extremely heavy.

Aquariums are only enclosed on five sides, so keepers have to purchase or build a suitable lid for the enclosure. After-market screen tops are available, but often, they are not secure enough for snakes.

Commercial Cages

Commercially produced cages have a number of benefits over other enclosures. Commercial cages usually feature doors on the front of the cage, allowing them to provide better access than top-opening cages do. Additionally, bypass glass doors or framed, hinged doors are generally more secure than after-market screened lids (as are used on aquariums) are.

Additionally, plastic cages are usually produced in dimensions that make more sense for snakes, and often have features that aid in heating and lighting the cage.

Commercial cages can be made out of wood, metal, glass or other substances, but the majority are PVC or ABS plastic.

Commercially cages are available in two primary varieties: those that are molded from one piece of plastic and those that are assembled from several different sheets. Assembled cages are less expensive and easier to construct, but molded cages have few (if any) seems or cracks in which bacteria and other pathogens can hide.

The sunbeam snake's flattened head helps them to burrow.

Some cage manufacturers produce cages in multiple colors. White is probably the best color for novices, as it is easy to see dirt, mites and other small problems. A single mite crawling on a white cage surface is very visible, even from a distance.

Black cages do not show dirt as well. This can be helpful for more experienced keepers who have developed proper hygiene techniques over time. Additionally, sunbeam snakes often look very sharp against black cage walls.

While some snakes have cone cells in their retinas, and can presumably see color, it is unlikely that cage color is a significant factor in their quality of life. If you worry about the selection of color, it is probably best to choose a dark or earth-toned color.

Plastic Storage Containers

Plastic storage containers, such as those used for shoes, sweaters or food, make suitable cages for snakes if they are customized to make them secure. The lids for plastic storage boxes are almost never secure enough to be used for sunbeam snakes without the addition of supplemental security measures.

Hobbyists and breeders overcome this by incorporating Velcro straps, hardware latches or other strategies into plastic storage container cages. While these can be secure, you must be sure they are 100 percent escape-proof before placing a snake in such cages.

The safest way to use plastic storage containers is with the use of a wooden or plastic rack. In such systems, often called "lidless" systems, the shelves of the rack form the top to the cage sitting below them. The gap between the top of the sides of the storage containers and the bottom of the shelves is usually very tight – approximately one-eighth inch or less.

When plastic containers are used, you must drill or melt numerous holes for air exchange. If you are using a lid, it is acceptable to place the holes in the lid; however, if you are using a lidless system, you will have to make the holes in the sides of the boxes.

All holes should be made from the inside towards the outside. This will help reduce the chances of leaving sharp edges inside the cage, which could cut the snake.

Homemade Cages

For keepers with access to tools and the desire and skill to use them, it is possible to construct homemade cages. However, this is not recommended for novice keepers, who do not yet have experience keeping snakes.

A number of materials are suitable for cage construction, and each has different pros and cons. Wood is commonly used, but must be adequately sealed to avoid rotting, warping or absorbing offensive odors.

Plastic sheeting is a very good material, but few have the necessary skills, knowledge and tools necessary for cage construction. Additionally, some plastics may have extended off-gassing times.

Glass can be used, whether glued to itself or with used with a frame. Custom-built glass cages can be better than aquariums, as you can design them in dimensions that are appropriate for snakes. Additionally, they can be constructed in such a way that the door is on the front of the cage, rather than the top.

Screen Cages

Screen cages make excellent habitats for some lizards and frogs, but they are poorly suited for most snakes. Screened cages do not retain heat well, and they are hard to keep suitably humid. Additionally, they are difficult to clean.

Screen cages are prone to developing week spots that can give sunbeam snake enough of a hole to push through and escape.

Chapter 7: Heating the Habitat

Providing the proper thermal environment is one of the most important aspects of reptile husbandry. As ectothermic ("cold-blooded") animals, sunbeam snakes rely on the surrounding temperatures to regulate the rate at which their metabolism operates.

Providing a proper thermal environment can mean the difference between a healthy, thriving pet and one who spends a great deal of time at the veterinarian's office, battling infections and illness.

While individuals may demonstrate slightly different preferences, and different species have slightly different preferences, most active sunbeam snakes prefer ambient temperatures in the low-80s Fahrenheit (between 26 and 29 degrees Celsius). Inactive (sleeping) sunbeam snakes prefer temperatures in the low 70s Fahrenheit (21 to 23 degrees Celsius).

However, while these are appropriate air temperatures for sunbeam snakes, they will also require a very warm basking spot during the day, with a temperature of about 85 degrees Fahrenheit (29 degrees Celsius).

Providing your sunbeam snake with a suitable thermal environment requires the correct approach, the correct heating equipment and the tools necessary for monitoring the thermal environment.

Size-Related Heating Concerns

Before examining the best way to establish a proper thermal environment, it is important to understand that your snake's body size influences the way in which he heats up and cools off.

Because volume increases more quickly than surface area does with increasing body size, small individuals experience more rapid temperature fluctuations than larger individuals do.

Accordingly, it is imperative to protect small individuals from temperature extremes. Conversely, larger sunbeam snakes are more tolerant of temperature extremes than smaller individuals are (though they should still be protected from temperature extremes).

Thermal Gradients

In the wild, sunbeam snakes move between different microhabitats so that they can maintain ideal body temperature as much as possible.

The best way to do this is by clustering the heating devices at one end of the habitat, thereby creating a basking spot (the warmest spot in the enclosure).

The temperatures will slowly drop with increasing distance from the basking spot, which creates a *gradient* of temperatures. Barriers, such as branches and vegetation, also help to create shaded patches, which provide additional thermal options.

This mimics the way temperatures vary from one small place to the next in your pet's natural habitat. For example, a wild sunbeam snakes may move under some vegetation to cool off at midday or move onto a sun-bathed rock to warm up in the morning.

By establishing a gradient in the enclosure, your captive snake will be able to access a range of different temperatures, which will allow him to manage his body temperature just as his wild counterparts do.

Adjust the heating device until the surface temperature at the basking spot is about 85 degrees Fahrenheit (29 degrees Celsius). It is probably a good idea to provide a slightly cooler basking spot for immature individuals.

Because there is no heat source at the other end of the cage, the ambient temperature will gradually fall as your snake moves away from the heat source. Ideally, the cool end of the cage should be in the low 70s Fahrenheit (22 degrees Celsius).

The need to establish a thermal gradient is one of the most compelling reasons to use a roomy cage. In general, the larger the cage, the easier it is to establish a suitable thermal gradient.

Heating Equipment

There are a variety of different heating devices you can use to keep your sunbeam snake's habitat within the appropriate temperature range.

Be sure to consider your choice carefully and select the best type of heating device for you and your pet.

Heat Lamps

Heat lamps are usually the best choice for supplying heat to your snake's habitat. Heat lamps consist of a reflector dome and an incandescent bulb. The light bulb produces heat (in addition to light) and the metal reflector dome directs the heat to a spot inside the cage.

You will need to clamp the lamp to a stable anchor or part of the cage's frame. Always be sure that the lamp is securely attached and will not be dislodged by vibration, children or pets.

Because fire safety is always a concern, and many keepers use high-wattage light bulbs, opt for heavy-duty reflector domes with ceramic bases, rather than economy units with plastic bases. The price difference is negligible, given the stakes.

One of the greatest benefits of using heat lamps to maintain the temperature of your pet's habitat is the flexibility they offer. While you can adjust the amount of heat provided by heat tapes and other devices with a rheostat or thermostat, you can adjust the enclosure temperature provided by heat lamps in two ways:

- Changing the Bulb Wattage

The simplest way to adjust the temperature of your pet's cage is by changing the wattage of the bulb you are using.

For example, if a 40-watt light bulb is not raising the temperature of the basking spot high enough, you may try a 60-watt bulb. Alternatively, if a 100-watt light bulb is elevating the cage temperatures higher than are appropriate, switching to a 60-watt bulb may help.

- Adjusting the Distance between the Heat Lamp and the Basking Spot

The closer the heat lamp is to the cage, the warmer the cage will be. If the habitat is too warm, you can move the light farther from the enclosure, which should lower the basking spot temperatures slightly.

However, the farther away you move the lamp, the larger the basking spot becomes. It is important to be careful that you do not move it too far away, which will reduce the effectiveness of the thermal gradient by heating the enclosure too uniformly. In very large cages, this may not compromise the thermal gradient very much, but in a small cage, it may eliminate the "cool side" of the habitat.

In other words, if your heat lamp creates a basking spot that is roughly 1-foot in diameter when it is 1 inch away from the screen, it will produce a slightly cooler, but larger basking spot when moved back another 6 inches or so.

Ceramic Heat Emitters

Ceramic heat emitters are small inserts that function similarly to light bulbs, except that they do not produce any visible light – they only produce heat.

Ceramic heat emitters are used in reflector-dome fixtures, just as heat lamps are. The benefits of such devices are numerous:

- They typically last much longer than light bulbs do

- They are suitable for use with thermostats

- They allow for the creation of overhead basking spots, as lights do

- They can be used day or night

However, the devices do have three primary drawbacks:

- They are very hot when in operation

- They are much more expensive than light bulbs

- You cannot tell by looking if they are hot or cool. This can be a safety hazard – touching a ceramic heat emitter while it is hot is likely to cause serious burns.

Radiant Heat Panels

Quality radiant heat panels are a great choice for heating most reptile habitats, including those containing sunbeam snakes. Radiant heat panels are essentially heat pads that stick to the roof of the habitat. They usually feature rugged, plastic or metal casings and internal reflectors to direct the infrared heat back into the cage.

Radiant heat panels have a number of benefits over traditional heat lamps and under tank heat pads:

- They do not produce visible light, which means they are useful for both diurnal and nocturnal heat production. They can be used in conjunction with fluorescent light fixtures during the day and remain on at night once the lights go off.

- They are inherently flexible. Unlike many devices that do not work well with pulse-proportional thermostats, most radiant heat panels work well with on-off and pulse-proportional thermostats.

The only real drawback to radiant heat panels is their cost: radiant heat panels often cost about two to three times the price of light- or heat pad-oriented systems. However, many radiant heat panels outlast light bulbs and heat pads, a fact that offsets their high initial cost over the long term.

Heat Pads

Heat pads are an attractive option for many new keepers, but they are not without drawbacks.

- Heat pads have a high risk of causing contact burns.

- If they malfunction, they can damage the cage as well as the surface on which they are placed.

- They are more likely to cause a fire than heat lamps or radiant heat panels are.

However, if installed properly (which includes allowing fresh air to flow over the exposed side of the heat pad) and used in conjunction with a thermostat, they can be reasonably safe. With heat pads, it behooves the keeper to purchase premium products, despite the small increase in price.

Heat Tape

Heat tape is somewhat akin to a "stripped down" heat pad. In fact, most heat pads are simply pieces of heat tape that have already been connected and sealed inside a plastic envelope.

Heat tape is primarily used to heat large numbers of cages simultaneously. It is generally inappropriate for novices and requires the keeper to make electrical connections. Additionally, a thermostat is always required when using heat tape.

Historically, heat tape was used to keep water pipes from freezing – not to heat reptile cages. While some commercial heat tapes have been designed specifically for reptiles, many have not. Accordingly, it may be illegal, not to mention dangerous, to use heat tapes for purposes other than for which they are designed.

Heat Cables

Heat cables are similar to heat tape, in that they heat a long strip of the cage, but they are much more flexible and easy to use. Many heat cables are suitable to use inside the cage, while others are designed for use outside the habitat.

Always be sure to purchase heat cables that are designed to be used in reptile cages. Those sold at hardware stores are not appropriate for use in a cage.

Heat cables must be used in conjunction with a thermostat, or, at the very least, a rheostat.

Nocturnal Temperatures

Because sunbeam snakes easily tolerate temperatures in the low-70s Fahrenheit (21 to 22 degrees Celsius) at night, most keepers can allow their pet's habitat to fall to ambient room temperature at night.

Because it is important to avoid using lights on your snake's habitat at night, those living in homes with lower nighttime temperatures will need to employ additional heat sources. Most such keepers accomplish this through the use of ceramic heat emitters.

Thermometers

It is important to monitor the cage temperatures very carefully to ensure your pet stays healthy. Just as a water test kit is an aquarist's best friend, quality thermometers are some of the most important husbandry tools for reptile keepers.

Ambient and Surface Temperatures

Two different types of temperature are relevant for pet sunbeam snakes: ambient temperatures and surface temperatures.

The ambient temperature in your animal's enclosure is the air temperature; the surface temperatures are the temperatures of the objects in the cage. Both are important to monitor, as they can differ widely.

Measure the cage's ambient temperatures with a digital thermometer. An indoor-outdoor model will feature a probe that allows you to measure the temperature at both ends of the thermal gradient at once. For example, you may position the thermometer at the cool side of the cage but attach the remote probe to a branch near the basking spot.

Because standard digital thermometers do not measure surface temperatures well, use a non-contact, infrared thermometer for such measurements. These devices will allow you to measure surface temperatures accurately from a short distance away.

Thermostats and Rheostats

Some heating devices, such as heat lamps, are designed to operate at full capacity for the entire time that they are turned on. Such devices should not be used with thermostats – instead, care should be taken to calibrate the proper temperature by tweaking the bulb wattage.

Other devices, such as heat pads, heat tape and radiant heat panels are designed to be used with a regulating device, such as a thermostat or rheostat, which maintains the proper temperature

Rheostats

Rheostats are similar to light-dimmer switches, and they allow you to reduce the output of a heating device. In this way, you can dial in the proper temperature for the habitat.

The drawback to rheostats is that they only regulate the amount of power going to the device – they do not monitor the cage temperature or adjust the power flow automatically. In practice, even with the same level of power entering the device, the amount of heat generated by most heat sources will vary over the course of the day.

If you set the rheostat so that it keeps the cage at the right temperature in the morning, it may become too hot by the middle of the day. Conversely, setting the proper temperature during the middle of the day may leave the morning temperatures too cool.

Care must be taken to ensure that the rheostat controller is not inadvertently bumped or jostled, causing the temperature to rise or fall outside of healthy parameters.

Thermostats

Thermostats are similar to rheostats, except that they also feature a temperature probe that monitors the temperature in the cage (or under the basking source). This allows the thermostat to adjust the power going to the device as necessary to maintain a predetermined temperature.

For example, if you place the temperature probe under a basking spot powered by a radiant heat panel, the thermostat will keep the temperature relatively constant at the basking site.

There are two different types of thermostats:

- On-Off Thermostats

On-Off Thermostats work by cutting the power to the device when the probe's temperature reaches a given temperature. For example, if the thermostat were set to 85 degrees Fahrenheit (29 degrees Celsius), the heating device would turn off whenever the temperature exceeds this threshold. When the temperature falls below 85, the thermostat restores power to the unit, and the heater begins functioning again. This cycle will continue to repeat, thus maintaining the temperature within a relatively small range.

Be aware that on-off thermostats have a "lag" factor, meaning that they do not turn off when the temperature reaches a given temperature. They turn off when the temperature is a few degrees above that temperature, and then turn back on when the temperate is a little below the set point. Because of this, it is important to avoid setting the temperature at the limits of your pet's acceptable range. Some premium models have an adjustable amount of threshold for this factor, which is helpful.

- **Pulse Proportional Thermostats**

Pulse proportional thermostats work by constantly sending pulses of electricity to the heater. By varying the rate of pulses, the amount of energy reaching the heating devices varies. A small computer inside the thermostat adjusts this rate to match the set-point temperature as measured by the probe. Accordingly, pulse proportional thermostats maintain much more consistent temperatures than on-off thermostats do.

Lights should not be used with thermostats, as the constant flickering may stress your pet. Conversely, heat pads, heat tape, radiant heat panels and ceramic heat emitters should always be used with either a rheostat or, preferably, a thermostat to avoid overheating your pet.

Thermostat Failure

If used for long enough, all thermostats eventually fail. The question is will yours fail today or twenty years from now. While some thermostats fail in the "off" position, a thermostat that fails in the "on" position may overheat your snake. Unfortunately, tales of entire collections being lost to a faulty thermostat are too common.

Accordingly, it behooves the keeper to acquire high-quality thermostats. Some keepers use two thermostats, connected in a series arrangement. By setting the second thermostat (the "backup thermostat") a few degrees higher than the setting used on the "primary thermostat," you safeguard yourself against the failure of either unit.

In such a scenario, the backup thermostat allows the full power coming to it to travel through to the heating device, as the temperature never reaches its higher set-point temperature.

However, if the first unit fails in the "on" position, the second thermostat will keep the temperatures from rising too high. The temperature will rise a few degrees in accordance with the higher set-point temperature, but it will not get hot enough to harm your pets.

If the backup thermostat fails in the "on" position, the first thermostat retains control. If either fails in the "off" position, the temperature will fall until you rectify the situation, but a brief exposure to relatively cool temperatures is unlikely to be fatal.

Chapter 8: Enclosure Furniture

Strictly speaking, it is possible to keep a sunbeam snake in a cage devoid of anything but a substrate that permits burrowing and a water bowl. However, complex environments, containing numerous climbing opportunities in the cage are preferable and will provide your snake with a higher quality of life.

Additionally, many keepers enjoy decorating the cage to resemble the animal's natural habitat. While such measures are not necessary from the snake's point of view, if implemented with care, there is no reason not to decorate your pet's cage, if you are inclined to do so.

However, it is recommended that beginners use a simple cage design for their first 6 to 12 months while they learn to provide effective husbandry.

Snakes will move about to find water, food, mates or appropriate environmental conditions. Each species (and individual) has a different typical activity level – some of the racers (*Coluber* sp.) and whip snakes (*Masticophis* sp.) may be accustomed to traveling many miles each day in search of food, but sunbeam snakes likely travel relatively little.

Hide Boxes

"Hide boxes" come in a wide variety of shapes, sizes and styles. Some keepers use modified plastic or cardboard containers, while others use realistic looking logs and wood pieces. Both approaches are acceptable, but all hides must offer a few key things:

- Hides should be safe for the snakes and feature no sharp edges or toxic chemicals.

- Hides should accommodate the snake, but not much else. They should be only slightly larger than the snake's body when it is laying in a flat coil.

- Hides should have low profiles. Snakes prefer to feel the top of the hide contacting the dorsal surface of their body.

- Hides either must be easy and economical to replace or constructed from materials that are easy to clean.

Plastic Storage Boxes

Just as a plastic storage box can be converted into an acceptable enclosure, small storage boxes can be converted into functional hiding places. Food containers, shoeboxes and butter tubs can serve as the base.

If the container has a low profile, it needs only have a door cut into the tub. Alternatively, you can discard the lid, flip the tub upside down and cut an entrance hole in the side.

Plant Saucers

The saucers designed to collect the water that overfills potted plants make excellent hiding locations. All you have to do is flip them upside down and cut a small opening in the side for a door.

Clay or plastic saucers can be used, but clay saucers are hard to cut. If you punch an entrance hole into a clay saucer, you must sand or grind down the edges to prevent hurting your snake.

Plates
Plastic, paper or ceramic plates make good hiding locations in cages that use particulate substrates. This will allow the snake to burrow up under the plate through the substrate and hide in a very tight space. Such hiding places also make it very easy to access your snake while he is hiding.

Cardboard Boxes
While you must discard and replace them anytime they become soiled, small cardboard boxes can also make suitable hide boxes. Just cut a hole in the side to provide a door.

Commercial "Half-Logs"
Many pet stores sell U-shaped pieces of wood that resemble half of a hollow log. While these are sometimes attractive looking items, they are not appropriate hide spots when used as intended.

The U-shaped construction means that the snake will not feel the top of the hide when he is laying inside. These hides can be functional if they are partially buried, thus reducing the height of the hide.

Cork Bark
Real bark cut from the cork oak (*Quercus suber*), "cork bark" is a wonderful looking decorative item that can be implemented in a variety of ways.

Usually cork bark is available in tube shape or in flat sheets. Flat pieces are better for sunbeam snakes. Flat pieces should only be used with particulate, rather than sheet-like substrates so that the snake can get under them easily.

Cork bark may be slightly difficult to clean, as its surface contains numerous indentations and crevices. Use hot water, soap and a sturdy brush to clean the pieces.

Commercially Produced Plastic Hides
Many different manufacturers market simple, plastic, hiding boxes. These are very functional if sized correctly, although some brands tend to be too tall. The simple design and plastic construction makes them very easy to clean.

Paper Towel Tubes
Small sections of paper towel tubes make suitable hiding spots for small sunbeam snakes. They do not last very long, so they require frequent replacement. They often work best if flattened slightly.

Newspaper or Paper Towels
Several sheets of newspaper or paper towels placed on top of the substrate (whether sheet-like or particulate) make suitable hiding spots.

Many professional breeders use paper-hiding spaces because it is such a simple and economically feasible solution. Some keepers crumple a few of the sheets to give the stack of paper more height.

Unusual Items
Some keepers like to express their individuality by using unique or unusual items as hiding spots. Some have used handmade ceramic items, while others have used skulls or

turtle shells. If the four primary criteria previously discussed are met, there is no reason such items will not make suitable hiding spaces.

Humid Hides

In addition to security, snakes also derive another benefit from many of their hiding spaces in the wild. Most hiding places feature higher humidity than the surrounding air.

By spending a lot of time in such places, snakes are able to avoid dehydration in habitats where water is scarce. Additionally, sleeping in these humid retreats aids in the shedding process. You should take steps to provide similar opportunities in captivity.

Humid hides can be made by placing damp sphagnum moss in a plastic container. The moss should not be saturated, but merely damp. You can also use damp paper towels or newspaper to increase the humidity of a hide box.

Some keepers prefer to keep humid hides in the habitat at all times, while others use them periodically – usually preceding shed cycles. Humid hides should never be the only hides available to the snake. Always use them in addition to dry hides.

Chapter 9: Substrates

Substrates are used to give your snake a comfortable surface on which to crawl and through which it can burrow. They also serve to absorb any liquids your snake releases.

There are a variety of acceptable choices, all of which have benefits and drawbacks. The only common substrate that is never acceptable is cedar shavings, which emits fumes that are toxic to snakes.

Just remember that whichever substrate you choose, it'll need to retain moisture well and provide your sunbeam snake with a relatively damp home. Sunbeam snakes will quickly suffer from a variety of health problems if kept in excessively dry conditions.

Nevertheless, it is wise to create a moisture gradient in your snake's habitat, just like you provide him with a thermal gradient. In other words, one side of his habitat should be kept damper than the other.

Some hobbyists go as far as to tilt their sunbeam snake's enclosure slightly, so that the "downhill" side of the habitat remains damper.

Paper Products

The easiest and safest substrates for sunbeam snakes are paper products in sheet form. While regular newspaper is the most common choice, some keepers prefer paper towels, unprinted newspaper, butcher's paper or a commercial version of these products.

Paper substrates are very easy to maintain, but they do not last very long and must be completely replaced when they are soiled. Accordingly, they must be changed regularly -- at least once per week.

Use several layers of paper products to provide sufficient absorbency and a little bit of cushion for the snake.

Many pet stores and pet supply retailers now carry recycled paper pulp products that can be used as bedding. Many keepers have used these substrates successfully, but they don't offer the primary benefits that sheet-style paper products do.

For example, they're not as easy to replace and they represent an ingestion hazard. They also cost significantly more than a few sheets of newspaper, so they haven't become as popular as some keepers predicted.

Nevertheless, despite the myriad benefits newspaper provides keepers, it is not the ideal substrate for sunbeam snakes, as it doesn't permit burrowing.

However, many keepers have used newspaper successfully, particularly once the snakes have adjusted to life in captivity.

If you decide to use newspaper for your sunbeam snakes habitat, be sure that you include a humid hide box in the enclosure too.

Pine Bark

Some hobbyists eschew pine, which is sometimes though to produce irritating fumes. While this may be true of products made from the xylem (wood) of pine trees, it is not true of products made from the bark.

Pine bark is not very absorbent, but it resists decay reasonably well. Pine bark is attractive and natural looking, but it does leave copious amounts of black dust inside the cage. It can be spot cleaned daily but requires monthly replacement.

Pine bark, like most other particulate substrates, does permit burrowing, so it offers particular value for those keeping sunbeam snakes.

Orchid Bark

The bark of fir trees is often used for orchid propagation, and so it is often called "orchid bark." Orchid bark is very attractive, though not quite as natural looking as pine bark. However, it exceeds pine in most other ways except cost.

Because orchid bark is often reddish in color, it is very easy to spot clean. However, monthly replacement can be expensive for those living in the eastern United States and Europe.

Like pine bark, orchid bark will allow your sunbeam snake to burrow extensively, so it is one of the best options available for those who can find it at a reasonable price.

Cypress Mulch

Cypress mulch is a popular substrate choice for many tropical species, and it helps to provide a moderately high humidity level. It also allows your snake to burrow.

One significant drawback to cypress mulch is that some brands (or individual bags among otherwise good brands) produce a stick-like mulch, rather than mulch composed of thicker pieces.

These sharp sticks can injure the keeper and the kept. It usually only takes one cypress mulch splinter jammed under a keeper's fingernail to cause them to switch substrates.

Cypress mulch is generally quite affordable, but you must be sure to select high-quality versions, which do not contain salvaged wood or other potentially dangerous items.

Soil

Organic potting soil or soil collected from a forested area can also be used in your sunbeam snake's enclosure. Both substrates are easy to acquire, affordable (or free) and retain moisture well, so they make excellent options.

Just be sure to collect the soil from an area that hasn't been exposed to pesticides or other chemicals, or, if you are purchasing the soil, opt for a variety that does not include perlite, fertilizers or other additives.

Chapter 10: Maintaining the Captive Habitat

Now that you have acquired your sunbeam snake and set up the enclosure, you must develop a protocol for maintaining his habitat. While sunbeam snake habitats require major maintenance every month or so, they only require minor daily maintenance.

In addition to designing a husbandry protocol, you must embrace a record-keeping system to track your sunbeam snake's growth and health.

Cleaning and Maintenance Procedures

Once you have decided on the proper enclosure for your pet, you must keep your sunbeam snake fed, hydrated and ensure that the habitat stays in proper working order to keep your captive healthy and comfortable.

Some tasks must be completed each day, while others are should be performed weekly, monthly or annually.

Daily

- Monitor the ambient and surface temperatures of the habitat.

- Spot clean the cage to remove any feces, urates or pieces of shed skin in the enclosure.

- Ensure that the lights, latches and other moving parts are in working order.

- Verify that your sunbeam snake is acting normally and appears healthy. You do not necessarily need to handle him to do so.

Weekly

- Change sheet-like substrates (newspaper, paper towels, etc.).

- Clean the inside surfaces of the enclosure.

- Inspect your sunbeam snake closely for any signs of injury, parasites or illness.

- Wash and sterilize all food dishes.

Monthly

- Break down the cage completely, remove and discard particulate substrates.

- Sterilize drip containers and similar equipment in a mild bleach solution.

- Measure and weigh your snake.

- Photograph your pet (recommended, but not imperative).

- Prune any plants present in the enclosure as necessary.

Annually

- Replace the batteries in your thermometers and any other devices that use them.

Cleaning your sunbeam snake's cage and furniture is relatively simple. Regardless of the way it became soiled, the basic process remains the same:

1. Rinse the object

2. Using a scrub brush or sponge and soapy water, remove any organic debris from the object.
3. Rinse the object thoroughly.
4. Disinfect the object.
5. Re-rinse the object.
6. Dry the object.

Chemicals & Tools

A variety of chemicals and tools are necessary for reptile care. Save yourself some time by purchasing dedicated cleaning products and keeping them in the same place that you keep your tools.

Spray Bottles

Occasionally misting your snake's cage will help ensure the enclosure doesn't become too dry. You can do this with a small, handheld misting bottle or a larger, pressurized unit (such as those used to spray herbicides). Automated units are available, but they are rarely cost-effective unless you are caring for a large colony of animals.

Small Brooms

Small brooms are great for sweeping up small messes and bits of substrate. It is usually helpful to select one that features angled bristles, as they'll allow you to better reach the nooks and crannies of your pet's cage and the surrounding area.

Ideally, the broom should come with its own dustpan to collect debris, but there are plenty of workarounds for those that don't come with their own.

Scrub Brushes or Sponges

It helps to have a few different types of scrub brushes and sponges on hand for scrubbing and cleaning different items. Use the least abrasive sponge or brush suitable for the task to prevent wearing out cage items prematurely. Do not use abrasive materials on glass or acrylic surfaces. Steel-bristled brushes work well for scrubbing coarse, wooden items, such as branches.

Spatulas and Putty Knives

Spatulas, putty knives and similar tools are often helpful for cleaning reptile cages. For example, urates (which are not soluble in anything short of hot lava) often become stuck on cage walls or furniture. Instead of trying to dissolve them with harsh chemicals, just scrape them away with a sturdy plastic putty knife.

Small Vacuums

Small, handheld vacuums are very helpful for sucking up the dust left behind from substrates. They are also helpful for cleaning the cracks and crevices around the cage doors. A shop vacuum, with suitable hoses and attachments, can also be helpful if you have enough room to store it.

Soap

Use a gentle, non-scented dish soap. Antibacterial soap is preferred, but not necessary. Most people use far more soap than is necessary -- a few drops mixed with a quantity of water is usually sufficient to help remove surface pollutants.

Bleach

Bleach (diluted to one-half cup per gallon of water) makes an excellent disinfectant. Be careful not to spill any on clothing, carpets or furniture, as it is likely to discolor the objects.

Always be sure to rinse objects thoroughly after using bleach and be sure that you cannot detect any residual odor. Bleach does not work as a disinfectant when in contact with organic substances; accordingly, items must be cleaned before you can disinfect them.

Veterinarian Approved Disinfectant

Many commercial products are available that are designed to be safe for their pets. Consult with your veterinarian about the best product for your situation, its method of use and its proper dilution.

Avoid Phenols

Always avoid cleaners that contain phenols, as they are extremely toxic to some reptiles. In general, do not use household cleaning products to avoid exposing your pet to toxic chemicals.

Keeping Records

It is important to keep records regarding your pet's health, growth and feeding, as well as any other important details. In the past, reptile keepers would do so on small index cards or in a notebook. In the modern world, technological solutions may be easier.

You can record as much information about your pet as you like, and the more information to you record, the better. But minimally, you should record the following:

Pedigree and Origin Information

Be sure to record the source of your sunbeam snake, the date on which you acquired him and any other data that is available. Breeders will often provide customers with information regarding the sire, dam, date of birth, weights and feeding records, but other sources will rarely offer comparable data.

Feeding Information

Record the date of each feeding, as well as the type of food item(s) offered. It is also helpful to record any preferences you may observe or any meals that are refused.

Note the sunbeam snake's small eyes.

Weights and Length

Because you look at your pet frequently, it is difficult to appreciate how quickly he is (or isn't) growing. Accordingly, it is important to track his size diligently.

Weigh your pet with a high-quality digital scale. It is often easiest to use a dedicated "weighing container" with a known weight to measure your pet. Simply subtract the weight of the container to obtain the weight of your snake.

You can also measure your snake's length as well, but it is not always easy to do so – snakes tend to wiggle quite a bit, which can make it difficult to keep them in a straight line without putting undo pressure on their body.

However, there are a number of web-based computer applications that will calculate the length of your snake if you take and upload a photo of him along with something of a known length (such as a ruler).

Maintenance Information

Record all of the noteworthy events associated with your pet's care. While it is not necessary to note that you misted the cage every other day, it is appropriate to record the dates on which you changed the substrate or sterilized the cage.

Whenever you purchase new equipment, supplies or caging, note the date and source. This not only helps to remind you when you purchased the items, but it may help you track down a source for the items in the future, if necessary.

Breeding Information

If you intend to breed your sunbeam snake, you should record all details associated with pre-breeding conditioning, cycling, introductions, matings, color changes, copulations and egg deposition.

Record all pertinent information about any resulting clutches as well, including the number of viable eggs, as well as the number of unhatched and unfertilized eggs.

Chapter 11: Feeding Sunbeam Snakes

For new keepers, few aspects of sunbeam snake care are as exciting as feeding their pet. However, feeding your pet properly entails more than just purchasing prey items and tossing them in your snake's cage periodically.

Instead, you must select the food items carefully, present the food items in a safe manner and do so on an appropriate schedule.

Prey Species

Sunbeam snakes consume a variety of different prey species in the wild, including rodents, frogs, lizards and other snakes. Most captive snakes will readily accept mice as food, and this is the best option for most keepers.

Freshly imported sunbeam snakes may require live mice for their first few meals. However, once they've begun feeding regularly, most will eagerly switch to frozen-thawed mice instead.

Prey Size

Sunbeam snakes have flexible jaws like most other snakes, but they are not capable of opening their mouths quite as wide as many other commonly kept pet species. So, you will need to feed your sunbeam snake slightly smaller prey than normal for snakes their size.

Ideally, the prey item should create a very small lump in the snake's body once swallowed. However, it is always better to err on the small side, if you have any doubt.

Typically, adult sunbeam snakes can handle small mice without problem, but there is nothing wrong with feeding them several mouse hoppers instead.

Feeding Quantity and Frequency

It's typically a good practice to feed sunbeam snakes about once every seven to ten days. You'll need to adjust the frequency of feedings to suit your snake's size and growth rate – subadults should exhibit a smooth, consistent growth rate, while adults should maintain a steady, healthy body weight.

Avoiding Regurgitation

Just like humans, snakes may regurgitate or vomit food items in response to a variety of stimuli, including toxins, stress and temperature extremes.

Accordingly, it is important to avoid causing the animal stress (especially right after meals) and maintaining the habitat within the correct temperature range.

Vomiting and regurgitation not only saddle the keeper with unpleasant clean up duties, they are very hard on the snake's body. Among other problems, vomiting can lead to dehydration and additional stress.

Give snakes that vomit at least one full week before offering food again. One of the biggest mistakes keepers make when dealing with a snake that has regurgitated is that they try to make up for the lost meal too quickly. This stresses the snake's digestive system and can lead to long-term, chronic problems

Chapter 12: Providing Water to Your Sunbeam Snake

Like most other animals, sunbeam snakes require drinking water to remain healthy. And while providing drinking water is a fairly straightforward task, there are a few things to keep in mind while doing so.

Providing Drinking Water

Most sunbeam snakes will readily drink from a water dish, so you'll want to provide your pet with a dish full of clean, fresh drinking water at all times.

While it is acceptable to offer the snakes a bowl that will accommodate the snake, it is not strictly necessary. Many keepers use bowls with 4- to 6-inch diameters. Be sure to avoid filling large containers too high, as they are apt to overflow if the snake crawls into the bowl.

Be sure to check the water dish daily and ensure that the water is clean. Empty, wash and refill the water dish any time it becomes contaminated with substrate, shed skin, urates or feces.

Some keepers prefer to use dechlorinated or bottled water for their snakes; however, untreated tap water is used by many keepers with no ill effects.

Misting to Maintain Humidity

Sunbeam snakes require a relatively high habitat humidity to remain healthy. One of the best ways to maintain a humid environment is by periodically misting the habitat with room-temperature water.

Most keepers will choose to do this each morning and allow the habitat to dry slightly over the following 24 hours.

If you'd rather not mist the habitat, you can just pour water directly into the substrate. However, care must be exercised, as you don't want to create excessively damp conditions.

Soaking Snakes

In addition to providing drinking water, many keepers soak their sunbeam snake periodically in a tub of clean, lukewarm water. Soaking is helpful tool for the husbandry of many snakes, and it helps to ensure proper hydration.

Additionally, soaks help to remove dirt and encourage complete, problem-free sheds. It is not necessary to soak your snake if it remains adequately hydrated, but most sunbeam snakes benefit from an occasional soak.

Soaks should last a maximum of about one hour and be performed no more often than once per week (unless the snake is experiencing shedding difficulties).

When soaking your snake, the water should not be very deep. Never make your snake swim to keep its head above water. Ideally, snakes should be soaked in containers with only enough water to cover their backs. This should allow your snake to rest comfortably with its head above water.

It is important to monitor your snake while he is soaking -- never leave a pet unattended while he is in a container of water. If your snake defecates in the water, be sure to rinse him off with clean water before returning him to his cage.

Chapter 13: Interacting with Your Sunbeam Snake

Many keepers enjoy handling pet snakes; assuming that they do not occur too frequently, gentle, brief handling sessions will rarely cause your pet much distress. However, sunbeam snakes are a little more easily stressed than many other species, so you'll want to keep handling to a minimum.

However, it will be necessary to handle your snake from time to time – not only so that you can move your pet when it becomes necessary to clean the cage, but also to monitor its health.

Every sunbeam snake is an individual, which means that different snakes respond differently when interacting with their keeper. Some will learn to tolerate gentle handling, while others will remain nervous throughout their lives.

No matter what side of the spectrum your snake falls on, you must be able to handle your pet when necessary.

Lifting a Sunbeam Snake

Try to move with a purpose once you open the cage door. Don't stare at your snake for 15 minutes as you try to work up your nerve. This often makes snakes feel insecure and increases their stress level.

Pick up your sunbeam snake by gently sliding your fingers underneath it and lifting its entire body into the air. Small snakes can be supported adequately with one hand, but two hands are necessary for lifting larger specimens.

Young sunbeam snakes can be flighty and nervous, but they usually calm down over time.

If you're nervous yourself, you can use a snake hook (or an improvised version thereof) to lift your snake from the ground. Strive to slip the hook under the snake near mid-body, lift it from the ground and transfer it to the intended location quickly.

Holding a Sunbeam Snake

Now that you have picked up your sunbeam snake, you must hold him in a way that prevents stress or injury.

The best way to hold a snake and keep it from feeling threatened is to provide it with plenty of support and allow it to crawl freely through your hands. Avoid restraining your snake or gripping it tightly with your hands, as this will cause it to feel like prey. Instead, simply support its body weight, and allow it to crawl from one hand to the other.

It is always wise to handle the snake over a table or other object to prevent his from falling to the floor, should he make a sudden move.

Transporting Your Pet

Although you should strive to avoid any unnecessary travel with your sunbeam snake, circumstances (such as illness) may demand that you do. Strive to make the journey as stress-free as possible for your pet. This means protecting him from physical harm, as well as blocking out any stressful stimuli.

The best type of container to use when transporting your snake is a plastic storage box. Add several ventilation holes to the container to provide suitable air exchange and be sure that the lid fits securely.

Place a few paper towels or some clean newspaper in the bottom of the box in case your snake defecates or discharges urates. It is also wise to crumple a few of the layers of newspaper, which will provide a place in which your snake can hide.

Cover the outside of the transport cage if you are not using an opaque container, which will prevent your pet from seeing the chaos occurring outside his container. Check up on your snake regularly but avoid constantly opening the container to take a peak. A quick peak once every half-hour or so is sufficient.

Pay special attention to the enclosure temperatures while traveling. Use your digital thermometer to monitor the air temperatures inside the transportation container. Try to keep the temperatures in the mid-70s Fahrenheit (23 to 25 degrees Celsius) so that your pet will remain comfortable.

Use the air-conditioning or heater in your vehicle as needed to keep the transport cage within this range (because you cannot control the thermal environment, it is not wise to take your snake with you on public transportation).

Keep your snake's transportation container stable while traveling. Do not jostle the container unnecessarily and always use a gentle touch when moving it. Never leave the container unattended.

Hygiene

Reptiles can carry *Salmonella* spp., *Escherichia coli* and several other zoonotic pathogens and parasites. Accordingly, it is imperative to use good hygiene practices when handling reptiles. Always wash your hands with soap and warm water each time you touch your pet, his habitat or the tools you use to care for him. Antibacterial soaps are preferred, but standard hand soap will suffice.

In addition to keeping your hands clean, you must also take steps to ensure your environment does not become contaminated with pathogens. In general, this means keeping your snake and any of the tools and equipment you use to maintain his habitat separated from your belongings.

Establish a safe place to prepare your pet's food, store equipment and clean his habitat. Make sure the place is far from places human food is prepared. Never wash cages or tools in kitchens or bathrooms that are used by humans. Always clean and sterilize any items that become contaminated by the germs from your snake or his habitat.

Chapter 14: Common Health Concerns

Like many other reptiles, sunbeam snakes are hardy animals, who often remain healthy despite their keeper's mistakes. In fact, most illnesses that befall pet sunbeam snakes result from improper husbandry, and are, therefore, entirely avoidable.

Nevertheless, like most other reptiles, sunbeam snakes often fail to exhibit any symptoms that they are sick until they have reached an advanced state of illness. This means that prompt action is necessary at the first hint of a problem. Doing so provides your pet with the greatest chance of recovery.

While proper husbandry is solely in the domain of the keeper, and some minor injuries or illnesses can be treated at home, veterinary care is necessary for many health problems.

Finding a Suitable Vet

While any veterinarian – even one who specializes in dogs and cats – may be able to help you keep your pet happy, it is wise to find a veterinarian who specializes in treating reptiles. Such veterinarians are more likely to be familiar with your pet species and be familiar with the most current treatment standards for reptiles.

Some of the best places to begin your search for a reptile-oriented veterinarian include:

- Veterinary associations

- Local pet stores

- Local colleges and universities

It is always wise to develop a relationship with a qualified veterinarian before you need his or her services. This way, you will already know where to go in the event of an emergency, and your veterinarian will have developed some familiarity with your pet.

When to See the Vet

Most conscientious keepers will not hesitate to seek veterinary attention on behalf of their pet. However, veterinary care can be expensive for the keeper and stressful for the kept, so unnecessary visits are best avoided.

If you are in doubt, call or email your veterinarian and explain the problem. He or she can then advise you if the problem requires an office visit or not.

However, you must always seek prompt veterinary care if your pet exhibits any of the following signs or symptoms:

- Traumatic injuries, such as lacerations, burns, broken bones or puncture wounds

- Sores, ulcers, lumps or other deformations of the skin

- Intestinal disturbances that do not resolve within 48 hours

- Drastic change in behavior

- Inability to deposit eggs

Remember that reptiles are perfectly capable of feeling pain and suffering, so apply the golden rule: If you would appreciate medical care for an injury or illness, it is likely that your pet does as well.

Common Health Problems

The following are some of the most common health problems that afflict sunbeam snakes. Be alert for any signs of the following maladies and take steps to remedy the problem.

Respiratory Infections

Respiratory infections are some of the most common illnesses that afflict sunbeam snakes and other captive reptiles.

The most common symptoms of respiratory infections are discharges from the nose or mouth; however, lethargy, inappetence and behavioral changes (such as basking more often than normal) may also accompany respiratory infections.

Myriad causes can lead to this type of illness, including communicable pathogens, as well as, ubiquitous, yet normally harmless, pathogens, which opportunistically infect stressed animals.

Your sunbeam snake may be able to fight off these infections without veterinary assistance, but it is wise to solicit your vet's opinion at the first sign of illness. Some respiratory infections can prove fatal and require immediate attention.

Your vet will likely obtain samples, send off the samples for laboratory testing and then interpret the results. Antibiotics or other medications may be prescribed to help your sunbeam snake recover, and your veterinarian will likely encourage you to keep the pet's stress level low and ensure his enclosure temperatures are ideal.

In fact, it is usually a good idea to raise the temperature of the basking spot upon first suspecting that your sunbeam snake is suffering from a respiratory infection. Elevated body temperatures (such as those that occur when mammals have fevers) help the pet's body to fight the infection, and many will bask for longer than normal when ill.

Internal Parasites

In the wild, most snakes carry some internal parasites. While it may not be possible to keep a snake completely free of internal parasites, it is important to keep these levels in check.

Consider any wild-caught snake to be parasitized until proven otherwise. While most captive bred snakes should have relatively few internal parasites, they can suffer from such problems as well.

Most internal parasites that are of importance for snakes are transmitted via the fecal-oral route. This means that eggs (or similar life stages) of the parasites are released with the feces. If the snake inadvertently ingests these, the resulting parasites can develop inside the snake's body and cause illness.

Such eggs are usually microscopic and easily lifted into the air, where they may stick to cage walls or land in the water dish. Later, when the snake flicks its tongue or drinks from the water dish, it ingests the eggs.

Because cages that are continuously contaminated from feces are likely to lead to dangerous parasite loads, employ strict hygiene practices at all times.

Internal parasites may cause your snake to vomit, pass loose stools, fail to grow or refuse food entirely. Other parasites may produce no symptoms at all, which illustrates the importance of routine examinations.

Your veterinarian will usually examine your snake's feces if he suspects internal parasites. By looking at the type of eggs inside the snake's feces, you veterinarian can determine which medication will treat the problem.

Many parasites are easily treated with anti-parasitic medications, but often, these medications must be given several times to eradicate the pathogens completely.

Some parasites may be transmissible to people, so always take proper precautions, including regular hand washing and keeping snakes and their cages away from kitchens and other areas where foods are prepared.

Examples of common internal parasites include roundworms, tapeworms and amoebas.

"Mouth Rot"
Mouth rot – properly called stomatitis – can be identified by noting discoloration, discharge or cheesy-looking material in the snake's mouth. Mouth rot can be a serious illness and requires the attention of your veterinarian.

While mouth rot often follows injury (such as happens when a snake strikes the side of a glass cage) it can also arise from systemic illness. Your veterinarian will cleanse your snake's mouth and potentially prescribe an antibiotic.

Your veterinarian may recommend withholding food until the problem is remedied. Always be sure that snakes that are recovering from mouth rot are kept in immaculately clean habitats with ideal temperature gradients.

External Parasites

The primary external parasites that afflict snakes are ticks and snake mites. Ticks are rare on captive bred animals, but wild caught snakes may be plagued by dozens of the small arachnids.

Ticks should be removed manually. Using tweezers grasp the tick as close as possible to the snake's skin and pull with steady, gentle pressure. Do not place anything over the tick first, such as petroleum jelly, or carry out any other "home remedies," such as burning the tick with a match. Such techniques may cause the tick to inject more saliva (which may contain diseases or bacteria) into the snake's body.

Drop the tick in a jar of isopropyl alcohol to kill it. It is a good idea to bring these to your veterinarian for analysis. Do not contact ticks with your bare hands, as many species can transmit disease to humans.

Mites are another matter entirely. While ticks are generally large enough to see easily, mites are about the size of a pepper flake. Whereas very bad tick infestations number in the dozens, mite infestations may include thousands of individual parasites.

Mites may afflict wild caught snakes, but, as they are not confined to a small cage, such infestations are somewhat self-limiting. In captivity, mite infestations can approach plague proportions.

After a female mite feeds on a snake, she drops off and finds a safe place (such as a tiny crack in a cage or among the substrate) to deposit her eggs. After the eggs hatch, they travel back to your snake (or to other snakes in your collection) where they feed and perpetuate the lifecycle.

Whereas a few mites may represent little more than an inconvenience to the snake, significant infestations can stress them considerably. In extreme cases, they may even lead to anemia and eventual death. This is particularly true for small or young animals. Additionally, mites may transmit disease from one snake to another.

There are a number of different methods for eradicating a mite infestation. In each case, there are two primary steps that must be taken: You must eradicate the snake's parasites and eradicate the parasites in the snake's environment (which includes the room in which the cage resides).

It is relatively simple to remove mites from a snake. When mites get wet, they die. However, mites are protected by a thick, waxy exoskeleton that stimulates the formation of an air bubble.

To defeat this waxy cuticle, you can simply add a few drops of liquid soap to the water. The soap will lower the surface tension of water, thereby preventing the air bubble from forming.

Soaking your snake is the slightly soapy water for about one hour will kill most of the mites on his body. Use care when doing so but try to arrange the water level and container so that most of the snake's body is below the water.

While the snake is soaking, perform a thorough cage cleaning. Remove everything from the cage, including water dishes, substrates and cage props. Sterilize all impermeable cage items and discard the substrate and all porous cage props. Vacuum the area around the cage and wipe down all of the nearby surfaces with a wet cloth.

It may be necessary to repeat this process several times to eradicate the mites completely. Accordingly, the very best strategy is to avoid contracting mites in the first place. This is why it is important to purchase your snake from a reliable breeder or retailer, and keep it quarantined from potential mite vectors.

Even if you purchase your snake from a reliable source, provide excellent husbandry and clean the cage regularly, you can end up battling mites if your friend brings his snake – which has a few mites – to your house.

It may even be possible for mites to crawl onto your hands or clothes, hop off when you return home and make their way to your snake.

Make it a practice to inspect your snake and his cage regularly. Look in the crease under the snake's lower jaw, near the eyes and near the vent -- common places in which mites hide. It can also be helpful to wipe down your snake with a damp, white paper towel. After wiping down the snake, observe the towel to see if any mites are present.

Chemical treatments are also available to combat mites, but you must be very careful with such substances. Beginners should rely on their veterinarian to prescribe or suggest the appropriate products to use.

Avoid repurposing lice treatments or other chemicals, as is often encouraged by other hobbyists. Such non-intended use may be very dangerous, and it is often in violation of Federal laws.

New hobbyists should consult with their veterinarian if they suspect that their snake has mites. Mite eradication is often a challenging ordeal that your veterinarian can help make easier.

Long-Term Anorexia

While short-term fasts of a few weeks are common among snakes, those that last longer than this may be cause for concern. If your snake refuses food, ensure that its habitat is set up ideally with ample hiding opportunities and access to appropriate temperatures.

If none of these factors requires attention, consult your veterinarian. Above all, do not panic – snakes can go very long periods of time without eating.

Your veterinarian will want to make sure that your snake is in good health, as respiratory infections, mouth rot or internal parasites may cause him to refuse food.

Some snakes refuse food in the winter or breeding season, as they would in the wild. While you should consult with your veterinarian the first time this happens, it shouldn't cause you much concern in subsequent years.

Injuries

Sunbeam snakes can become injured in myriad ways. While they are likely to heal from most minor wounds without medical attention, serious wounds will necessitate veterinary assistance.

Your vet will likely clean the wound, make any repairs necessary and prescribe a course of antibiotics to help prevent infection. Be sure to keep the enclosure as clean as possible during the healing process.

Egg Binding

Egg binding occurs when a female is unable or unwilling to deposit her eggs in a timely fashion. If not treated promptly, death can result.

The primary symptoms of egg binding are similar to those that occur when a gravid sunbeam snake approaches parturition. Egg bound sunbeam snakes may explore their egg deposition chamber incessantly or attempt to escape their enclosure. However, unlike snakes who will deposit eggs normally, egg bound sunbeam snakes continue to exhibit these symptoms without producing a clutch of eggs.

As long as you are expecting your sunbeam snake to lay eggs, you can easily monitor her behavior and act quickly if she experiences problems. However, if you are not anticipating a clutch, this type of problem can catch you by surprise.

Prolapse

Prolapses occur when a sunbeam snake's intestines protrude from its vent. This is an emergency situation that requires prompt treatment. Fortunately, intestinal prolapse is not terribly common among sunbeam snakes.

You will need to take the animal to the veterinarian, who will attempt to re-insert the intestinal sections. Sometimes sutures will be necessary to keep the intestines in place while the muscles regain their tone.

Try to keep the exposed tissue damp, clean and protected while traveling to the vet. It is likely that this problem is very painful for the animal, so try to keep its stress level low during the process.

Skin Blisters

Sunbeam snakes often develop blisters when kept in excessively dry conditions. Unfortunately, these blisters – which can prove fatal if not treated – strongly resemble those that occur in snakes who are kept in excessively damp conditions.

This leads many keepers to utilize dry habitats in hopes of treated their sunbeam snake. This is obviously counterproductive, and results in an even sicker snake.

Speak with your vet if your snake develops skin blisters and heed the advice given. Just be sure to mention that sunbeam snakes often suffer these blisters from excessively dry conditions, as relatively few vets will be familiar with sunbeam snakes.

Quarantine

Quarantine is the practice of isolating animals to prevent them from transferring diseases between themselves.

If you have no other pet reptiles (particularly other sunbeam snakes), quarantine is unnecessary. However, if you already maintain other sunbeam snakes you must provide all new acquisitions with a separate enclosure.

At a minimum, quarantine all new acquisitions for 30 days. However, it is wiser still to extend the quarantine period for 60 to 90 days, to give yourself a better chance of discovering any illness present before exposing your colony to new, potentially sick, animals. Professional zoological institutions often quarantine animals for six months to a year. In fact, some zoos keep their animals in a state of perpetual quarantine.

Chapter 15: Breeding Sunbeam Snakes

Many snake keepers are intrigued at the idea of breeding their snakes. While this is a fun, educational activity, you must be sure that you understand the risks and responsibilities that accompany such attempts.

For example, it is sometimes necessary to allow some snake species to brumate in order to instigate breeding behaviors. Exposing your animal to reduced temperatures makes them more susceptible to illness. When their body temperatures are low, snakes' immune systems do not work as effectively as normal. If your snakes become sick during the brumation period, they will require immediate veterinary attention.

Other problems may occur as well; males may suffer damaged hemipenes or females may become egg bound. Either of which may be fatal without prompt treatment. You may find it necessary to take your pet to the veterinarian for costly treatment – potentially without any guarantee of success.

If you manage to get through the entire process without problem, you will one day find eggs that require incubation. If this is successful, you will find yourself caring for a dozen or more other snakes. While it is possible to sell them, this is not as easy as it sounds, and rarely generates profit.

Many municipalities require expensive permits to keep large numbers of snakes – selling them requires other permits altogether. You will have to learn how to ship snakes and obtain the necessary permits for that. Additionally, you will have to spend money to advertise that you have snakes for sale. Ultimately, most beginners find that it is simply best to give away the snakes to other keepers.

Finally, you must consider the costs associated with housing a large number of hatchlings. Each will need its own habitat, heat supply and water dish, as they cannot be housed together.

Nevertheless, and unlike most other popular pet snake species, sunbeam snakes are very rarely bred in captivity. Achieving captive reproduction is quite difficult, and few beginners are likely to succeed.

Keepers have yet to establish a method or set of techniques that consistently results in viable eggs. Accordingly, captive reproduction will take considerable experimentation.

The approach detailed below is based on a generalized plan that is often effective for eliciting reproduction in other snakes, but there is no guarantee it will work with sunbeam snakes.

Pre-Cycling Conditioning

Only snakes in perfect health should be considered for breeding trials. If a snake exhibits signs of stress, respiratory illness, mites, mouth rot or other illnesses, avoid breeding the snake or engaging in cycling until the snake is 100 percent health.

During the late summer and early fall, feed adults slated for breeding trials heavily. However, avoid allowing either animal to become overweight – overweight snakes make poor breeders.

Thermal- and Photo-Cycling

It isn't clear whether or not sunbeam snakes require and temperature or photo (daylight) cycling to achieve successful reproduction.

Their natural habitats rarely become very cold during the winter, and those hailing from the southernmost portions of their range may not experience much of a "winter" at all.

If you decide to lower the habitat temperatures to cycle your animals, only do so gradually. Additionally, you'll only want to drop the habitat temperatures a few degrees – drastic temperature drops (such as those used when breeding many temperate snakes) are likely to cause illness.

Pairing

Following a very slight cooling period, you can restore the habitats normal temperatures. You can begin introducing the snakes together at this time.

It is always wise to observe snakes when you introduce them to each other – particularly when it is the first time two snakes have met. Some snakes just are not compatible, and may engage in antagonistic behaviors or fight. This can lead to serious injuries or death if the subordinate animal cannot escape.

Some breeders prefer to place males in the females' cages, while others prefer the opposite. Still others use a neutral cage, unique to both.

Pairs may begin copulating minutes after you place them in the same cage, or they may never breed if they are not compatible. Generally, snakes are housed together until they copulate, and then they are separated and fed, if they will eat.

Reintroduce the snakes periodically to allow further mattings and increase the chances for fertile eggs. When the pair stops showing interest, halt the introductions.

Post-Partum Care and Egg Deposition

After several copulations, the female can be kept by herself and fed regularly. Always offer smaller-than-normal food items at this time, to reduce the chances of disrupting the reproductive processes.

A few weeks after successful mating, the female will ovulate. Snakes have two ovaries, which may release ova at the same time or individually, a few days apart. When snakes ovulate, all of the ova in a given ovary are released simultaneously, allowing them to move into the oviducts, where they are shelled and eventually deposited a few weeks later.

Ovulation may create a dramatic mid-body swelling in the female. It can be much larger than the bulge caused by a typical food item, or it can be small enough to go unnoticed. However, ovulation marks an important reference point when trying to prepare for the ensuing eggs.

Most snakes shed once between the time of ovulation and egg deposition. About two to four weeks after this shed (depending on the species); the female will deposit the eggs. Accordingly, you must provide her with an egg-laying box when she is about to shed.

The egg-laying box is similar to a hide box, but it includes some moss, mulch or newspaper in the bottom. Different breeders prefer different substrates for the box, but there is likely little difference between the various options.

The egg-laying medium should be very slightly damp, but not wet. Err on the side of dryness, to avoid problems with mold, bacteria and fungi.

Once the female has finished depositing the eggs, she will often leave them, as sunbeam snakes do not practice any maternal care. You can generally reach in the cage and remove the entire egg box at this point.

Allow the female to rest and rehydrate for about 24 hours, and then offer her food. Most females eat ravenously at this time to help replenish their energy stores.

The Incubator

You can either purchase a commercially produced incubator or construct your own. However, most beginning breeders are better served by purchasing a commercial incubator than making their own.

Commercial Incubators

Commercial egg incubators come in myriad styles and sizes. Some of the most popular models are similar to those used to incubate poultry eggs (these are often available for purchase from livestock supply retailers).

These incubators are constructed from a large foam box, fitted with a heating element and thermostat. Some models feature a fan for circulating air; while helpful for maintaining a uniform thermal environment, models that lack these fans are acceptable.

You can place an incubation medium directly in the bottom of these types of incubators, although it is preferable to place the media (and eggs) inside small plastic storage boxes, which are then placed inside the incubator.

These incubators are usually affordable and easy to use, although their foam-based construction makes them less durable than most premium incubators are.

Other incubators are constructed from metal or plastic boxes; feature a clear door, an enclosed heating element and a thermostat. Some units also feature a backup thermostat, which can provide some additional protection in case the primary thermostat fails.

These types of incubators usually outperform economy, foam-based models, but they also bear higher price tags. Either style will work, but, if you plan to breed snakes for many years, premium models usually present the best option.

Homemade Incubators

Although incubators can be constructed in a variety of ways, using many different materials and designs, two basic designs are most common.

The first type of homemade incubator consists of a plastic, glass or wood box, and a simple heat source, such as a piece of heat tape or a low-wattage heat lamp. The heating source must be attached to a thermostat to keep the temperatures consistent. A thermometer is also necessary for monitoring the temperatures of the incubator.

Some keepers make these types of incubators from wood, while others prefer plastic or foam. Although glass is a poor insulator, aquariums often serve as acceptable incubators; however, you must purchase or construct a solid top to retain heat.

Place a brick on the bottom of the incubator and place the egg box on top of the brick, so that the eggs are not resting directly on the heat tape. The brick will also provide thermal mass to the incubator, which will help maintain a more consistent temperature.

The other popular incubator design adds a quantity of water to the design to help maintain consistent temperatures and a higher humidity. To build such a unit, begin with an aquarium fitted with a glass or plastic lid.

Place a brick in the bottom of the aquarium and add about two gallons of water to the aquarium; ideally, the water level should stop right below the top of the brick.

Add an aquarium heater to the water and set the thermostat to the desired temperature. Place the egg box on the brick, insert a temperature probe into the egg box and cover the aquarium with the lid (you may need to purchase a lid designed to allow the cords to pass through it).

This type of incubator works by heating the water, which will in turn heat the air inside the incubator, which will heat the eggs. Although it can take several days of repeated adjustments to get these types of incubators set to the exact temperature you would like, they are very stable once established.

Incubation Conditions

Before removing the eggs from the egg-laying box, mark the top of each egg with a graphite pencil. This is necessary because the tiny snake embryo attaches to the inside of the eggshell at an early stage in development. If the egg is rotated after this happens, the young animal can drown inside the egg.

After marking the tops, gently remove the eggs and transfer them to the egg incubation box. Do not use force to separate any eggs that are attached – while experienced breeders often separate such eggs, the risk of destroying some of them is high. Simply place clumps of attached eggs in the egg incubation box in the same orientation in which they are in the deposition box.

Place the eggs in the incubation box in the same orientation in which they were deposited in the egg-laying box. Bury the eggs about halfway in the vermiculite.

There are many different opinions regarding the best place to install the thermostat's temperature probe. Some prefer placing it in the main incubator chamber, while others prefer to place the probe inside the egg box.

Place the egg incubation box inside the incubator and close it tightly. Do not inspect the eggs too frequently, as this may cause unnecessary temperature spikes.

No one knows the optimal incubation temperatures or the average amount of time required to incubate them. However, most probably hatch in about 60 days when incubated around 80 degrees Fahrenheit (26 degrees Celsius).

Hatchling Husbandry

Establish "nursery cages" for the young snakes about a week before the eggs should hatch. The container should contain only a bit of slightly damp substrate, a very shallow water dish and a few places to hide (crumpled newspaper works well).

Keep the nursery very clean, slightly humid and at about 80 degrees Fahrenheit (26 degrees Celsius), 24-hours a day. The hatchlings do not need much light – that coming in the side of the nursery is ample. Do not handle the hatchlings unless necessary, until they are about one month old and eating well.

It is not uncommon for hatchlings to emerge with their yolks still attached. Do not attempt to remove or separate the tissue in such situations; doing so could cause severe injury or death to the hatchling. Instead, simply keep the hatchling in a nursery cage and ensure that the tissue does not dry out. Generally, by keeping the nursery slightly humid, the tissue will remain moist and dethatch on in its own in a few days.

Hatchlings usually shed several weeks after they hatch. At this point, you can place them in habitats that are like small versions of the adult cages.

Give them a few days to settle in and begin offering food. Some experienced keepers prefer to offer food as soon as possible after shedding, but others prefer to wait. In either case, your snake has energy reserves that will sustain them for several weeks, so there is no need to rush the process.

Chapter 16: Further Reading

Never stop learning more about your new pet's natural history, biology and captive care. This is the only way to ensure that you are providing your new snake with the highest quality of life possible.

It's always more fun to watch your sunbeam snake than read about him, but by accumulating more knowledge, you'll be better able to provide him with a high quality of life.

Books

Bookstores and online book retailers offer a treasure trove of information that will advance your quest for knowledge. While books represent an additional cost involved in reptile care, you can consider it an investment in your pet's well-being. Your local library may also carry some books about sunbeam snakes, which you can borrow for no charge.

University libraries are a great place for finding old, obscure or academically oriented books about snakes. You may not be allowed to borrow these books if you are not a student, but you can view and read them at the library.

Herpetology: An Introductory Biology of Amphibians and Reptiles
By Laurie J. Vitt, Janalee P. Caldwell
Top of Form
Bottom of Form
Academic Press, 2013

Understanding Reptile Parasites: A Basic Manual for Herpetoculturists & Veterinarians
By Roger Klingenberg D.V.M.
Advanced Vivarium Systems, 1997

Infectious Diseases and Pathology of Reptiles: Color Atlas and Text
Elliott Jacobson
CRC Press

Designer Reptiles and Amphibians
Richard D. Bartlett, Patricia Bartlett
Barron's Educational Series

Magazines

Because magazines are typically published monthly or bi-monthly, they occasionally offer more up-to-date information than books do. Magazine articles are obviously not as comprehensive as books typically are, but they still have considerable value.

Reptiles Magazine

www.reptilesmagazine.com/

Covering reptiles commonly kept in captivity.

Practical Reptile Keeping

http://www.practicalreptilekeeping.co.uk/

Practical Reptile Keeping is a popular publication aimed at beginning and advanced hobbies. Topics include the care and maintenance of popular reptiles as well as information on wild reptiles.

Websites

The internet has made it much easier to find information about reptiles than it has ever been.

However, you must use discretion when deciding which websites to trust. While knowledgeable breeders, keepers and academics operate some websites, many who maintain reptile-oriented websites lack the same dedication to scientific rigor.

Anyone with a computer and internet connection can launch a website and say virtually anything they want about sunbeam snakes. Accordingly, as with all other research, consider the source of the information before making any husbandry decisions.

The Reptile Report
www.thereptilereport.com/

The Reptile Report is a news-aggregating website that accumulates interesting stories and features about reptiles from around the world.

Kingsnake.com
www.kingsnake.com

After starting as a small website for gray-banded kingsnake enthusiasts, Kingsnake.com has become one of the largest reptile-oriented portals in the hobby. The site features classified advertisements, a breeder directory, message forums and other resources.

The Vivarium and Aquarium News

www.vivariumnews.com/

The online version of the former print publication, The Vivarium and Aquarium News provides in-depth coverage of different reptiles and amphibians in a captive and wild context.

Journals

Journals are the primary place professional scientists turn when they need to learn about snakes. While they may not make light reading, hobbyists stand to learn a great deal from journals.

Herpetologica

www.hljournals.org/

Published by The Herpetologists' League, Herpetologica, and its companion publication, Herpetological Monographs cover all aspects of reptile and amphibian research.

Journal of Herpetology

www.ssarherps.org/

Produced by the Society for the Study of Reptiles and Amphibians, the Journal of Herpetology is a peer-reviewed publication covering a variety of reptile-related topics.

Copeia

www.asihcopeiaonline.org/

Copeia is published by the American Society of Ichthyologists and Herpetologists. A peer-reviewed journal, Copeia covers all aspects of the biology of reptiles, amphibians and fish.

Nature
www.nature.com/

Although Nature covers all aspects of the natural world, many issues contain information that sunbeam snake enthusiasts are sure to find interesting.

Supplies

You can obtain most of what you need to maintain snakes through your local pet store, big-box retailer or hardware store, but online retailers offer another option.

Just be sure that you consider the shipping costs for any purchase, to ensure you aren't "saving" yourself a few dollars on the product yet spending several more dollars to get the product delivered.

Big Apple Pet Supply
http://www.bigappleherp.com

Big Apple Pet Supply carries most common husbandry equipment, including heating devices, water dishes and substrates.

LLLReptile
http://www.lllreptile.com

LLL Reptile carries a wide variety of husbandry tools, heating devices, lighting products and more.

Doctors Foster and Smith
http://www.drsfostersmith.com

Foster and Smith is a veterinarian-owned retailer that supplies husbandry-related items to pet keepers.

Support Organizations

Sometimes, the best way to learn about sunbeam snakes is to reach out to other keepers and breeders. Check out these organizations, and search for others in your geographic area.

The National Reptile & Amphibian Advisory Council
http://www.nraac.org/

The National Reptile & Amphibian Advisory Council seeks to educate the hobbyists, legislators and the public about reptile and amphibian related issues.

American Veterinary Medical Association
www.avma.org

The AVMA is a good place for Americans to turn if you are having trouble finding a suitable reptile veterinarian.

The World Veterinary Association
http://www.worldvet.org/

The World Veterinary Association is a good resource for finding suitable reptile veterinarians worldwide.

References

Aldridge, D. S. (2011). Controversial snake relationships supported by reproductive anatomy. *Journal of Anatomy*.

ALEXANDRE TEYNIÉ, P. D. (2015). A new genus and species of xenodermatid snake (Squamata: Caenophidia: Xenodermatidae) from northern Lao People's Democratic Republic. *Zootaxa*.

Anderson, S. P. (2003). The Phylogenetic Definition of Reptilia. *Systematic Biology*.

Arnold, S. J. (1972). Species Densities of Predators and Their Prey. *The American Naturalist*.

Bergman, R. (1955). The anatomy of Xenopeltis unicolor. *Zoologische Mededelingen*.

Chandi, M. (2006). The Use and Knowledge of Herpetofauna on Little Nicobar Island, India. *Conservation and Society*.

Frazzetta, T. (1999). Adaptations and significance of the cranial feeding apparatus of the sunbeam snake (Xenopeltis unicolor): Part I. Anatomy of the skull. *Journal of Morphology*.

Grandison, A. G. (1977). Snakes of West Malaysia and Singapore. *Annalen des Naturhistorischen Museums in Wien*.

Jeffrey C. Beane, S. P. (2013). Published by: The American Society of Ichthyologists and Herpetologists. *Copeia*.

Kooij, D. P. (1996). Scale Sensillae of the File Snake (Serpentes: Acrochordidae) and Some Other Aquatic and Burrowing Snakes. *Netherlands Journal of Zoology*.

NICOLAS VIDAL, A.-S. D. (n.d.). THE HIGHER-LEVEL RELATIONSHIPS OF ALETHINOPHIDIAN SNAKES INFERRED FROM SEVEN NUCLEAR AND MITOCHONDRIAL GENES. In *Biology of Boas and Pythons*.

SAVITZKY, A. H. (1981). Hinged Teeth in Snakes: An Adaptation for Swallowing Hard-Bodied Prey. *Science*.

TOMÁŠ SCHOLZ, A. D. (2013). Macrobothriotaenia ficta (Cestoda: Proteocephalidea), a parasite of sunbeam. *Zootaxa*.

Index

Anorexia, 91
Aquariums, 38
Bleach, 69
Breeding, 72
cage, 36, 37, 38, 39, 40, 41, 42, 45, 48, 49, 50, 63, 86, 89, 90, 91
Cleaning, 65, 66
Cork Bark, 58
Cypress Mulch, 64
Dimensions, 36
eggs, 84, 92, 93, 100, 101, 102
Feeding, 70, 74
Glass cages, 38
Heat, 46, 47, 48, 49, 50
Heat Cables, 50
Heat Pads, 49
Heat Tape, 49
Homemade Cages, 41
Humid Hides, 60
husbandry, 107, 109, 110
mites, 88, 89, 90, 91

Mouth rot, 87
Newspaper, 59
online, 105
Orchid Bark, 63
Paper Towels, 59
Pine, 63
plastic storage boxes, 41
Prey, 73
probe, 51
Regurgitation, 74
Rheostats, 52
Screen Cages, 42
Security, 38
Temperature, 43
Temperatures, 51
Thermal Gradients, 44
Thermometers, 51
Thermostats, 52
veterinarian, 35, 43, 69, 87, 88, 91, 92, 110
veterinarian's, 43
Water, 77

Copyright and Trademarks: This publication is Copyrighted 2018 by Zoodoo Publishing. All products, publications, software and services mentioned and recommended in this publication are protected by trademarks. In such instance, all trademarks & copyright belong to the respective owners. All rights reserved. No part of this book may be reproduced or transferred in any form or by any means, graphic, electronic, or mechanical, including photocopying, recording, taping, or by any information storage retrieval system, without the written permission of the authors. Pictures used in this book are either royalty free pictures bought from stock-photo websites or have the source mentioned underneath the picture.

Disclaimer and Legal Notice: This product is not legal or medical advice and should not be interpreted in that manner. You need to do your own due-diligence to determine if the content of this product is right for you. The author and the affiliates of this product are not liable for any damages or losses associated with the content in this product. While every attempt has been made to verify the information shared in this publication, neither the author nor the affiliates assume any responsibility for errors, omissions or contrary interpretation of the subject matter herein. Any perceived slights to any specific person(s) or organization(s) are purely unintentional. We have no control over the nature, content and availability of the web sites listed in this book. The inclusion of any web site links does not necessarily imply a recommendation or endorse the views expressed within them. Zoodoo Publishing takes no responsibility for, and will not be liable for, the websites being temporarily unavailable or being removed from the Internet. The accuracy and completeness of information provided herein and opinions stated herein are not guaranteed or warranted to produce any particular results, and the advice and strategies, contained herein may not be suitable for every individual. The author shall not be liable for any loss incurred as a consequence of the use and application, directly or indirectly, of any information presented in this work. This publication is designed to provide information in regards to the subject matter covered. The information included in this book has been compiled to give an overview of the subject s and detail some of the symptoms, treatments etc. that are available to people with this condition. It is not intended to give medical advice. For a firm diagnosis of your condition, and for a treatment plan suitable for you, you should consult your doctor or consultant. The writer of this book and the publisher are not responsible for any damages or negative consequences following any of the treatments or methods highlighted in this book. Website links are for informational purposes and should not be seen as a personal endorsement; the same applies to the products detailed in this book. The reader should also be aware that although the web links included were correct at the time of writing, they may become out of date in the future.

www.ingramcontent.com/pod-product-compliance
Lightning Source LLC
Chambersburg PA
CBHW071715040426
42446CB00011B/2082